# Holy Listening

*The Art of Spiritual Direction*

Margaret Guenther

COWLEY PUBLICATIONS
*Cambridge* ♦ *Boston*
*Massachusetts*

© 1992 Margaret Guenther
All rights reserved.

Published in the United States of America by Cowley Publications, a division of the Society of St. John the Evangelist. No portion of this book may be reproduced, stored in or introduced into a retrieval system, or transmitted, in any form or by any means—including photocopying—without the prior written permission of Cowley Publications, except in the case of brief quotations embodied in critical articles and reviews.

International Standard Book Number: 1-56101-056-1
Library of Congress Number: 91-44746

**Library of Congress Cataloging-in-Publication Data**
Guenther, Margaret, 1929 -
Holy Listening : the art of spiritual direction / Margaret Guenther.
p. cm.
1. Spiritual direction. 2. Women—Religious Life. 3. Guenther, Margaret, 1930 -   . I. Title.
BV5053.G84   1992
253.5'3—dc20                    91-44746

All biblical quotations are taken from the *New Revised Standard Version*.

This book is printed on acid-free paper and was produced in the United States of America.

*Tenth Printing*

*Cowley Publications*
*28 Temple Place*
*Boston, Massachusetts 02111*

For P.B.

Cowley Publications is a ministry of the Society of St. John the Evangelist, a religious community for men in the Episcopal Church. Emerging from the Society's tradition of prayer, theological reflection, and diversity of mission, the press is centered in the rich heritage of the Anglican Communion.

Cowley Publications seeks to provide books, audio cassettes, and other resources for the ongoing theological exploration and spiritual development of the Episcopal Church and others in the body of Christ. To this end, it is dedicated to developing a new generation of theological writers, encouraging them to produce timely, creative, and stimulating publications of excellence, and making these publications available widely, reaching both clergy and lay persons.

# Acknowledgments

I am grateful to the trustees of the General Theological Seminary and to my faculty colleagues for the gift of time that enabled me to write this book.

I am also grateful to Daniel Warren, who brought me together with Cowley Publications and its editor, Cynthia Shattuck. From working with her, I have learned that good editors have a great deal in common with good spiritual directors: she has been a midwife, teacher, and generous host.

Finally, I thank Alan Jones, whose friendship and encouragement helped me to find my voice.

# Table of Contents

*Preface by Alan Jones*     *ix*

Introduction
*Holy Listening*     *1*

Chapter One
*Welcoming the Stranger*     *7*

Chapter Two
*Good Teachers*     *41*

Chapter Three
*Midwife to the Soul*     *81*

Chapter Four
*Women and Spiritual Direction*     *109*

Epilogue     *141*

# Preface

Some years ago, a monk responded angrily (but with a twinkle in his eye) to a lecture I had given on spiritual direction. I don't think he was mad at me or even at the subject matter. It was the trendiness of it all that got to him. He said, "What I want is some non-spiritual non-direction!" He had a point. Spiritual direction can easily become too "spiritual" in the sense of being ungrounded and unreal. It can become too directive by either being overly clinical or authoritarian. There is always the danger of the well-meaning or spiritually bossy charging into someone's life uninvited and doing some real damage. Some of us like to dabble in other people's lives and thus enlarge ourselves by interfering.

Spiritual direction needs demystifying and Margaret Guenther goes a long way to do just that by writing a wise and penetrating book about non-spiritual non-direction. She has managed to throw light on the ordinary ground of everyday human experience out of which extraordinary acts of spiritual courage and perseverance are born.

In some ways, the art of spiritual direction lies in our uncovering the obvious in our lives and in realizing that everyday events are the means by which God tries to reach us. When Molière's Bourgeois Gentilhomme discovered that all language was either poetry or prose, he was delighted to learn that he had been speaking prose all his life without knowing it. So with us. All along we've had a spiritual life and we didn't know it. There *is* poetry in the spiritual life but most of the time we are living in the prosaic mode.

# HOLY LISTENING
*The Art of Spiritual Direction*

Margaret Guenther knows a great deal about the strange ministry of gracious human interaction that the tradition calls the midwifery of the soul. She also knows that writing about spiritual direction can be hazardous. It has become a mini-industry in religious publishing. This is all right in itself. The danger lies in the fact that it is well-nigh impossible not to be infected by the prevailing attitudes of an acquisitive, competitive, and consumer society. These attitudes even permeate our approach to things spiritual. Prayer is one more thing one has to *do*, one more skill one has to learn in order to run the spiritual race and get ahead. For some, having a spiritual director is like having your own shrink or your own personal trainer at the gym. It gives one spiritual status. It promises a spiritual edge over others. Having a spiritual director is like moving out of the inner city of the spirit and into the suburbs where there are more facilities and the promise of a membership in the country club of the soul. Having a spiritual mentor will make you spiritually upwardly mobile.

Another debilitating effect of the drive and greed of a consumer society on the life of the spirit is the assumption that everything is, in principle, *fixable*. True spiritual direction is about the great unfixables in human life. It's about the mystery of moving through time. It's about mortality. It's about love. It's about things that can't be fixed. Margaret Guenther knows about the great unfixables.

Talk about spiritual direction can, therefore, be very irritating. It's not so much the subject matter per se as the fact that when we talk about anything "spiritual" resentment, jealousy, and guilt are often stirred up in people—partly because we are haunted by the specter of unfixability. If someone implies that he or she has anything approaching a disciplined spiritual life, some of us get a sinking feeling inside. We either compare ourselves unfavorably with the other person, or we look for the flaws that must be hiding under the veneer of piety.

What kind of person, therefore, should be writing about the spiritual life today? She would need to be very grounded in ordinary, everyday experience. She would need to be earthy and have the ability to see the funny side of the spiritual enterprise even in the midst of great suffering. She would need to be crafty—wily enough to spot the byzantine ploys of the ego to make itself the center of everything, even of its own suffering and struggle. She would need to be able to make judgments without being judgmental, to smell a rat without allowing her ability to discern deception sour her vision of the glory and joy that is everyone's birth-right in God. Margaret Guenther is such a writer. She is also a feminist, that is, she writes from the perspective of a woman who has known what it is to be made invisible and to be set aside, ignored and unheard.

There's a lot of daft talk about the need for "a woman's perspective." One writer recently told of the way in which she was always called upon for "the woman's point of view" in graduate school. It became an in-joke with her friends: "Speaking as a woman, I think I'll have meatloaf for dinner." Yet there *is* a much-neglected feminine perspective that is at last being heard. Margaret writes a great deal about listening, waiting, and presence—all attributes that are associated with the feminine. She is unafraid of using images traditionally associated almost exclusively with women—metaphors of housekeeping and house-cleaning. But she pulls no punches when she takes on patriarchal attitudes and posturing. When it comes to matters of simple injustice and plain ecclesiastical nonsense, she is both critical and inclusive.

Spiritual direction is very susceptible to the female imagery of pregnancy and birth-giving. God is the great birth-helper. It is no wonder that midwifery is the overriding metaphor of spiritual direction, and Margaret Guenther insists that men are as capable of it as women. We assist at the birth of each other in an environment of gracious hospitality. We also, from time to time, act as parents to each other. When a formerly autistic child was asked what parents were for,

HOLY LISTENING
*The Art of Spiritual Direction*

she replied, "They hope for you." That is what we can do for each other.

But there is more to be learned than the recovery of the feminine in the use of metaphors from midwifery. There is also the recovery of the role of older people (the elders) in bringing souls to term. Grandmothers and grandfathers can play an important part in soul-making. Margaret conjures up the image of the Appalachian granny woman—wise, resourceful, and experienced—assisting at the birth of babies in cottages and shacks remote and hard to reach. We need spiritual grannies and grandpas who have the time and the wisdom to wait patiently in out-of-the-way places of the spirit and quietly bring new things to birth in others.

Men and women have common sins but they also have ones very much identified with their particular sex. The traditional sin is pride and it is still very much alive, but, according to Margaret Guenther, the sin that clings particularly to women is that of self-contempt. Man's pride and woman's self-contempt (while not exclusive to either sex) make relations between the sexes unusually sour at the moment. Perhaps that is why both men and women invoke a high and cruelly idealistic standard of behavior that only superbeings could uphold. Modern secular standards of morality are draconian compared to the old-fashioned religious standards which, at least, held out the promise of forgiveness. Most of us make a fundamental error with regard to the nature of morality itself. We all want a workable framework of rules in a fixable world that most of us can follow without any real effort. We like things to work, including our morality. So we try to maneuver ourselves into a morally secure position by changing the rules. The new rules are either a device to punish the politically incorrect or so inconsequential that human relations are trivialized.

There is another point of view that this book will do a great deal to revive. This other perspective is best illustrated by reference to a story of an encounter between a Catholic convert from communism and one of his old atheist colleagues. "The difference between us is that I believe in absolute responsibility and absolute forgiveness. You believe in no responsibility and no forgiveness." Human life isn't worth living without our willingly accepting responsibility for our behavior, yet that would be too heavy a burden without the possibility of forgiveness. Those of us who hope for a more caring and humane world had better be aware of forgiveness (both human and divine) if we are going to navigate the stormy seas of human relations. Much of the pain could be avoided if we knew how to frame questions about our longings and were willing to forgive one another, even as we seek to make one another accountable. Spiritual direction, at its best, does just this.

The spiritual director has the double task of holding up the demands of absolute responsibility and the promise of absolute forgiveness. It is out of such demands and promises that we assist at each other's birth. Margaret Guenther knows what it means to grow into being someone. There is waiting, stillness, and hope. "When in doubt," she writes, "I always assume that God is at work, that is, the person is pregnant." Just as she found it useful to refer to *The Complete Book of Midwifery*, so her readers will find this book an invaluable manual in recognizing God's amazing work in us and among us in the ordinariness of human existence. In the very best sense, hers is a book on non-spiritual non-direction: earthed and wise, compassionate and unsentimental, practical and contemplative. May more of us be willing to seek hospitality with another in the art of birth-giving.

Alan Jones
*Grace Cathedral, San Francisco*

# Holy Listening

This is a book by an amateur, written for amateurs. "Amateur" is a word that has been devalued in our time, connoting someone not to be taken seriously, not quite up to snuff, certainly a poor (but usually inexpensive) substitute for the worthy professional.

Yet the amateur is one who loves, loves the art that she serves, loves and prays for the people who trust her, loves the Holy Spirit who is the true director in this strange ministry called spiritual direction. The amateur is nervous about hanging up a shingle or taking an ad in the Yellow Pages, and waits instead for others to name his gift, may even find out quite accidentally his calling to this ministry. With Abba Macarius of the fourth-century Egyptian desert, who protested, "I have not yet become a monk myself, but I have seen monks," the amateur-lover-director may say, "Who, me? I have not yet become a spiritual director myself, but I have seen spiritual directors."[1]

It is a strange ministry, often exercised in the cracks, intruding itself into the practicalities of parish administration or sermon-writing or teaching. Sometimes I am almost reluctant to name it, for the very words—spiritual direction—can be offputting or seductive, as they conjure up the image of a clerical Svengali compelling a trembling soul to kneel on broken glass while reciting the *Miserere*.

Domination and submission are not what spiritual direction is about, but "holy listening," presence and attentiveness. Thinking about listening makes me remember Mrs. G from my days as a hospital chaplain. A formidable woman who looked like the Red Queen in *Alice*, she was seriously ill

HOLY LISTENING
*The Art of Spiritual Direction*

and—with her ceaseless demands—a source of annoyance to the nursing staff. One day after I had fetched her glasses and found her teeth, adjusted the television and repaired the Venetian blind, put fresh water in her pitcher and plumped her pillow, I assumed that Mrs. G had run out of urgent needs. But she beckoned me close and said, "One more thing. Get me out of here!" When I protested that, much as I would like her to be well, granting this particular request was out of my power, Mrs. G looked at me with disappointment and some disgust. "You mean you just walk around and listen to people?" I felt very small and very fake when I answered, "I'm afraid that's it, Mrs. G." A slow smile crept over the Red Queen's face. "Well, I guess that's work, too."

I don't walk around much any more, but I still listen a lot. And I often think of Mrs. G, who probably never heard of spiritual direction but would no doubt grudgingly recognize that "it was work, too."

Paradoxically, the need and hunger are there, even as we struggle to define the ministry. Cursillo has brought the words "spiritual direction" back into currency, but most lay people and many clergy are uneasy and unsure of their significance in the late twentieth-century church. We are hungry, and we don't know for what. We want something, but we can't name it. The parish is taking good care of us, nourishing us with word and sacrament, just as the hospital made sure that Mrs. G was fed, nursed, and medicated. But we want something else, something more: we want to be touched, we want to be known as children of God. All too often we miss the point, assuming like Mrs. G that adjustment of the external environment will somehow fix everything. Yet what we really hunger for is wholeness and God.

The spiritual director may be tempted to fix things, to be diverted as I was by details like teeth and glasses, television and window shades. To combat such temptation, it is good to remember the spiritual maxim offered by John Irving in one of his novels: when you help people, you mess with them. Anthony the Great had a similar idea over 1600 years earlier,

2

*Introduction*
HOLY LISTENING

when he quoted Abba Paphnutius as saying, "I have seen a man on the bank of the river buried up to his knees in mud and some men came to give him a hand to help him out, but they pushed him further in up to his neck." Anthony commented approvingly of Paphnutius: "Here is a real man, who can care for souls and save them."[2] Whatever we do as spiritual directors, we are neither to mess with them nor push them further into the mud.

Yet the hunger is there, and some of us—lay and ordained—find ourselves asked to respond. Again and again, people call for an appointment "to talk to somebody." There is urgency in their voices, and they are often surprised that no one can see them that very day, that it might be necessary to wait a week or two. Then, when they arrive, when the door is finally shut and the phone turned off, they say apologetically, "I'm not really sure why I'm here. I don't know what I want." They want God, of course, but they aren't able to say so. They want to know themselves in relation to God, but they aren't able to say that either. They want spiritual direction, but that, too, they are often unable to say.

Spiritual direction is not psychotherapy nor is it an inexpensive substitute, although the disciplines are compatible and frequently share raw material. Spiritual direction is not pastoral counseling, nor is it to be confused with the mutuality of deep friendships, for it is unashamedly hierarchical. Not because the director is somehow "better" or "holier" than the directee, but because, in this covenanted relationship the director has agreed to put himself aside so that his total attention can be focused on the person sitting in the other chair. What a gift to bring to another, the gift of disinterested, loving attention!

In the pages that follow, I will attempt to describe the shape that spiritual direction might take for people of our time, aware that the subject is an elusive one. I am speaking to the beginner, those persons lay or ordained, with or without formal theological training, who find themselves drawn to this ministry. Perhaps they feel the stirring of their

HOLY LISTENING
*The Art of Spiritual Direction*

own unacknowledged gifts. Or perhaps they wonder about receiving direction, whether it is a ministry available to "ordinary people" or reserved for the especially holy. I hope some dark corners will be illuminated and some questions answered.

As an amateur, I can write only from my own perspective. First and foremost, this is the perspective of a woman, a woman who has been married for over three decades and who has borne and reared children. Most of the major recent books on spiritual direction have been written by men—the names of Alan Jones, Morton Kelsey, Tilden Edwards, William Barry, William Connolly, Kenneth Leech, and Martin Thornton come immediately to mind—although Edwards points out that women appear to have special gifts for this ministry:

> My suspicion is that there are many more great women spiritual guides than the record shows, but who have remained in obscurity in the normative dominance of men in the positions of visible leadership....My own experience points to more potentially gifted women than men as spiritual companions.[3]

Furthermore, a number of the women who *do* write on the subject as members of religious orders and hence speak from a different life experience and viewpoint. My life as a women, wife, and mother has given my ministry its particular shape.

I also write from the perspective of a teacher, as one who has spent a lifetime entrusted with the minds and lives of students. I have always been aware, at some level, of the holiness of the teacher's vocation. With each passing year, the connections become clearer to me: teaching is indeed ministry, and much ministry—especially the ministry of spiritual direction—is teaching.

Finally, I write as a priest of the Episcopal Church. When I first sought ordination, I was sure that my ministry lay with the dying, most probably in the institutional ministry of hospital, nursing home, or hospice. To find myself again in

*Introduction*
HOLY LISTENING

academe seemed at first ironic to me, a sign of divine humor, but upon reflection, very right. I do indeed work with the dying, for we are all dying, and helping in the preparation for a good death is priestly work.

To be asked by someone to serve as spiritual director is an expression of great trust and my immediate reaction is almost always, "Am I up to this? What makes this person think that I am worthy of his trust?"

It is my hope that in this book no trust has been violated and that my pledge of confidentiality has been observed. But this work would not be possible without the very real people who sit with me in my office or who ask for conferences during retreats and quiet days I conduct. Because of them, I am not writing about what spiritual direction might or should be, but about one person's ministry as it really is. So all of the stories I have told are *true*, but not necessarily *factual*. No real names are used, circumstances have been changed, and composites created. Since this is a book about "ordinary" direction situations, there are many commonalities. While each person seeking direction is unique, there are recurrent motifs, problems, and concerns. The *sameness* is far from boring; it is part of the human condition, binding us together and enabling us to feel kinship with the great spiritual writers, once we have got past the superficialities that make them seem remote.

I am deeply grateful to my directees, my spiritual children who are my brothers and sisters, my fellow travelers, and my friends. I thank all of you: women and men; gay, lesbian, and straight; tentative seekers and confident theologians; young and old. If you think you recognize yourself in these pages, you do—and you don't. In some instances, when the story becomes very specific and the material is delicate, I have secured your permission. In others, your story is here, woven—I hope—seamlessly and discreetly into the fabric.

# Endnotes

1 Benedicta Ward, *The Desert Christian: The Sayings of the Desert Fathers* (New York: Macmillan, 1975), p. 125.

2 *Ibid.*, p. 7.

3 Tilden Edwards, *Spiritual Friend: Reclaiming the Gift of Spiritual Direction* (New York: Paulist, 1980), p. 67.

CHAPTER ONE

# Welcoming the Stranger

He looked up and saw three men standing near him. When he saw them, he ran from the tent entrance to meet them, and bowed down to the ground. He said, "My lord, if I find favor with you, do not pass by your servant. Let a little water be brought, and wash your feet, and rest yourselves under the tree. Let me bring a little bread, that you may refresh yourselves, and after that you may pass on—since you have come to your servant." So they said, "Do as you have said." And Abraham hastened into the tent to Sarah, and said, "Make ready quickly three measures of choice flour, knead it, and make cakes." And Abraham ran to the herd, and took a calf, tender and good, and gave it to the servant, who hastened to prepare it. Then he took curds and milk, and the calf that he had prepared, and set it before them; and he stood by them under the tree while they ate.
*Genesis 18:2-8*

Do not neglect to show hospitality to strangers, for by doing that some have entertained angels without knowing it.
*Hebrews 13:2*

Let all guests who arrive be received like Christ, for He is going to say, "I came as a guest, and you received Me."
*Rule of St. Benedict (Chapter 53)*

# Welcoming the Stranger

Every morning my day begins with a look at the little black appointment book. Usually the space is crowded with names and phone numbers, and the shape of the day is predictable. But occasionally the name scribbled in is unfamiliar to me: someone is coming for the first time, presumably to explore the possibility of spiritual direction, but even that is not always clear. I'm not always sure how the person found me—a suggestion from the parish clergy, a casual reference by a friend of a friend, the grapevine, or even the New York telephone book. Despite a preliminary phone conversation to set up the appointment, we are strangers to each other, names without faces or stories.

I am about to show hospitality to a stranger, a prospect simultaneously exhilarating and disquieting. I become self-conscious; they are expecting someone older, younger, taller, shorter, at least someone who looks like a spiritual director. While my friends and colleagues are used to my office with its books and pictures, will a stranger be put off? And what about this stranger? What does he want of me? Will he be interesting, tedious, challenging, or—this is, after all, New York—deranged? These thoughts do not always run through my mind in clear sequence, but they hover just beneath the surface when a potential directee presents himself for the first time. I feel my kinship with Abraham when he lifted up his eyes and beheld three strangers standing in front of him. My guest, like his, has paused on a journey. Do I really want to stop what I am doing and invite him to wash his feet and rest under the tree before he passes on? Geographically, the journey is rarely impressive—a subway ride from uptown, a

*Chapter One*
## WELCOMING THE STRANGER

commuter train trip from New Jersey, a five-minute walk through the seminary close. The person standing at my office door is rarely disheveled or dust-covered and would resist any attempt of mine to wash his feet. But spiritually, he has come a great distance and is still far from home.

Like all of us, the person seeking spiritual direction is on a journey. Since the expulsion from Eden, we have been a people on the move, despite attempts at self-delusion that we have somehow arrived, We follow in the footsteps of our peripatetic Lord, always on the way, our faces turned resolutely or reluctantly toward Jerusalem. Mobility is our way of life. How many of us live within ten, even one hundred miles of our birthplace? And how many of us have any idea where we will die? Physically, our life is a journey. Spiritually, too, we are always on the way, *in via*, when we long to be *in patria*. We are travelers, and we are weary and homesick.

It is a fact of life that travelers cannot survive in comfort without hospitality. However prudent their planning and abundant their supplies, if the journey goes on long enough they will need the care of a host, someone who offers a temporary home as a place of rest and refreshment. Thus Abraham offered water for his angelic visitors to wash the dust from their feet, fresh-baked bread and meat to ease their hunger. Thus, too, McDonald's golden arches and the familiar logo of the Holiday Inn beckon us, promising dubious refreshment and bland surroundings. (The best surprise is no surprise, we are told. On the spiritual journey, the reverse might well be true!) Even the most self-sufficient cannot escape this need for hospitality: modest recreational vehicle and splendiferous mobile home alike turn into those discreetly labelled areas in national parks that invite them to empty their waste tanks before continuing on.

In the harsh circumstances of the desert or the frontier, hospitality offers more than comfort: it also ensures physical survival. Spiritually, too, we cannot make it through the desert or across the frontier alone, but must depend on the kindness of strangers. Yet those strangers upon whom we depend are not really strangers, but our sisters and brothers in Christ. They are the hosts, the givers of hospitality, who sustain us on the journey, our spiritual friends and directors.

"Host" is a word with many connotations, not all of them comfortable in the context of a discussion of spiritual direction. Talk shows have hosts—yet one would scarcely think of Johnny Carson or David Letterman as bestowers of hospitality in the biblical sense. Flight attendants used to be called hostesses, pretty young women who made sure that passengers were buckled into immobility before distributing drinks and little plastic containers of plastic food. A grim and sterile vision of hospitality!

Perhaps English speakers have devalued the word "host." Certainly it lacks the freshness and immediacy of the German *Gastgeber*—the guest-giver, the one who gives to guests—and *Gastfreundschaft*—guest-friendship, the special friendship shown by hosts to their guests. The spiritual director is a host who gives to her guests, the bestower of guest-friendship. She is a host in the truest and deepest sense, reflecting the abundant hospitality shown by the host at the heavenly banquet.

*Getting Ready*

Anyone who has ever given a dinner party or entertained weekend guests knows that hospitality is hard work, made even harder by the necessity that it appear effortless. Abraham had it easy: while he greeted his guests effusively, offering them the best that he has, his servant was butchering and dressing the calf, and Sarah was scurrying around inside the tent making cakes. For most of us nowadays, and certainly for those who practice spiritual direction as a ministry of hospitality, it is not so easy to delegate the real (i.e. tedious and painstaking) work to others. but the first step in being a good host, for dinner or for spiritual direction, is to get ready, to have the preparation done so that the scurrying may cease and the guest be greeted graciously.

*Chapter One*
## WELCOMING THE STRANGER

Guests provide a helpful discipline. Left on our own, we can walk endlessly around disorder and uncleanness, vowing to do something about the state of our house some time, but not now. We may even come to love our untended garbage, to treasure it or at least to take it for granted. But when an honored guest is coming, we carry out the trash, restore objects to their places, and create an uncluttered, clean, and welcoming space. So it is also for spiritual directors. The first task is one of housecleaning, of creating our own inner order. We must know ourselves well, both our dark corners and our airless places—the spots where dust collects and mold begins to grow. It is not enough to push our rubbish into the closet and shut the door, nor to lower blinds and dim the lights so that the dirt doesn't show, although these are tempting tricks for harried caretakers of houses and of souls. No, we must clean our house, and then keep cleaning it so that we have a worthy place when we invite others to rest and refreshment.

Literal housecleaning is tiresome but straightforward work; scrubbing and polishing bear visible results that we can see and admire. Spiritual housecleaning is more subtle and cannot be done alone. Anyone presuming to undertake this ministry without the guidance of her own director is embarking on a dangerous path of self-deception, the spiritual equivalent of jamming all the junk into an out-of-the-way closet or shoving it down the cellar stairs to be dealt with later.

So the first step for any director is, with help, to become self-aware. Spiritually, the house must be kept in order, at least to the degree that it offers a wholesome and not a dangerous environment to those who shelter there.

Trusting in my own director, I must be willing to leave my own safe place and seek hospitality with another, to ask for help and let myself be guided. I must be willing to be the needy, vulnerable, weary traveler as well as the generous host. It is easier to be the host, as Abba James of the desert knew, when he said, "It is better to receive hospitality than to

# HOLY LISTENING
*The Art of Spiritual Direction*

offer it."[1] <u>Having a spiritual director keeps me honest, makes me aware of the corners of neglect, and helps me keep the house reasonably tidy.</u>

Spiritual directors need all the help they can get if they are to maintain themselves in a reasonable state of fitness. (No one expects perfection!) In addition to a director of one's own, we all need spiritual friends with whom we can speak of our deepest concerns, and who do not fear to speak the truth in love to us. The unofficial patron saint of spiritual directors, Aelred of Rievaulx, wrote in the twelfth century:

> A man is to be compared to a beast if he has no one to rejoice with him in adversity, no one to whom to unburden his mind if any annoyance crosses his path or with whom to share some unusually sublime or illuminating inspiration....He is entirely alone who is without a friend.
>
> But what happiness, what security, what joy to have someone to whom you dare to speak on terms of equality as to another self; one to whom you can unblushingly make known what progress you have made in the spiritual life; one to whom you can entrust all the secrets of your heart and before whom you can place all your plans.[2]

I had never heard of Aelred when I first met my friend Janet, but later I recognized her in his words. She is English, a musician and a medievalist as well as a sensitive lay theologian. She gives me something I cannot give myself. Except for her disapproval of my fondness for florid, late nineteenth-century Russian piano music, she accepts and loves me as I am. I value her keen mind and uncompromising honesty; and although we have never analyzed it, I know that our friendship is equally valuable to her. Distance keeps us from meeting oftener than once a year, but each time there is a sense of homecoming and complete safety. There is no place for the trivial in our conversations, nor any place for pious posturing. While we rarely pray together, our talk is always God-talk as we "speak on terms of equality as to another self."

*Chapter One*
## WELCOMING THE STRANGER

There are also those things we can do for ourselves, and that keep us ready to receive guests. I find the personal journal a great aid in self-awareness. There are methods and disciplines of journal-keeping, some so formidable that they discourage all but the most zealous. A free-form, "write when you need to" system works well for me. By keeping the journal in looseleaf binders, I am able to write on the typewriter or word processor and to include letters, poems, and articles that have become part of my story. Journal entries can be made at any time and any place, then carried home to be placed in the binder. Once I decided that no one would read it or, if they did, it wouldn't matter since I would be dead, I have been able to write candidly. In the journal, you can be as repetitive as you wish; it is a place to wrestle with angels and struggle with demons.

Retreat time also helps in maintaining a healthy perspective. A retreat is not synonymous with a vacation; the former has an intentional austerity. The radically simplified environment discourages inner clutter. In most religious houses there is "nothing to do"—no games, no distractions, no loud noises, no TV, no busyness. Instead, there is silence, simple food, adequate space, and the security of being surrounded by a praying community. For those of us who get trapped in crowded schedules and fall into the dangerous and sinful delusion that we, the administrative assistants of a well-meaning but inefficient CEO God, are really the ones who hold up the world, even a brief retreat is a powerful corrective. When we have slowed down, we are able to look at ourselves and smile at our pitiful little constructs. Our humility is restored; at least for a little while, we are reminded of our true place in the order of things.

Spiritual directors, confessors, spiritual friends, and retreats—all quite *spiritual* ways of keeping our house in order! Yet it is very easy to overlook the more ordinary gifts of creation as aids to wholeness. Blessed are those who number babies and animals among their friends; in their embodied innocence, such small creatures keep us simple.

# HOLY LISTENING
## The Art of Spiritual Direction

Blessed are those who find God's hand in the aesthetic: music, literature, and art keep us joyful and proportionate. And blessed are those who enjoy good, hard work. There is nothing like sawing through a log or mowing a lawn, scrubbing a *very* dirty floor or kneading a loaf of bread to make us rejoice in our physicality and bring us close to the earth. A spiritual director who becomes too "spiritual" is more than a little frightening.

### Sharing our space

What happens when we offer hospitality? We invite someone into a space that offers safety and shelter and put our own needs aside, as everything is focused on the comfort and refreshment of the guest. For a little while at least, *mi casa es tu casa*, as the Spanish gracefully puts it. There are provisions for cleansing, food, and rest. Hospitality is an occasion for storytelling with both laughter and tears, and then the guest moves on, perhaps with some extra provisions or a roadmap for the next stage of the journey.

At its simplest, hospitality is a gift of space, both physical and spiritual, and like the gift of attentive listening, it is not to be taken lightly. This is brought home to me every day when I go to work. I live in New York, where the population density contributes to stress, even to the high degree of violence, and where one quickly becomes aware of the invisible lines that secure a modicum of psychological privacy. Thus one learns to avoid eye contact in the subway and to move briskly along crowded pavements, coming within millimeters of fellow pedestrians but without actually *touching* anyone. Space is treasured, guarded jealously.

But as spiritual directors, we gladly share our space, the outer space of study or office and the inner space where God can met. Unlike the New Yorker on the crowded street, we do not fear being generous with our territory nor do we fear intimacy with another person. We offer the best we have.

Physical space is, in its way, as important as spiritual space. I find that I cannot see people for spiritual direction in

*Chapter One*
## WELCOMING THE STRANGER

my home: there is too much confusion of roles and personae. Even if family members and pets can be banished to other parts of the house, the impedimenta of daily living intrude and make the space so personal that our appointment threatens to turn into a friendly chat. To meet in the directee's home is even less satisfactory, unless illness, age, or frailty makes it difficult to come to us. Most public places, such as restaurants, are also problematic—how can you be meaningfully silent together when the waiter wants to tell you his name and recite the specials of the day? Park benches are fine in good weather, and empty churches are a weekday resource. However, a quiet room that is pleasant and uncluttered, personal but not overly so, is preferable. Most of my work as a director is done in my office, a spacious and sunny room in an early nineteenth-century building. (I am told that in gentler times it housed the seminary infirmarian, a connection I find appropriate and comforting.) Before a meeting, I try to arrange the chaos on the desk into tidy piles and to push the word processor into its unobtrusive corner, minimal gestures of transforming "business" space into "holy" space.

When I first occupied this office, I recoiled from the rug that delineated the "conversation area" of the room. The chairs were all right, quite comfortable and not too bad to look at. But the rug! When I looked at the unfortunate red plaid that had seen better days, with visibly worn spots and tears on its edges, I vowed that it would have to go as soon as the budget would permit a replacement. But now that rug has become an important part of my offer of hospitality. Again and again, in the silence at the beginning of a session, I hear in my heart the words from Aelred: "Here we are, you and I, and I hope a third, Christ, is in our midst." At some point, and I am not sure when, a place in the middle of that red plaid rug became holy. Even with the most lavish budget, I could never replace it now. Only last week, a directee arrived from another city and said, "You know, all the way on the train I kept seeing your rug!"

# HOLY LISTENING
*The Art of Spiritual Direction*

The space offered for spiritual direction should be as welcoming as possible: icons, a plant or a few flowers, gentle light, a comfortable temperature, and quiet all contribute. More importantly, though, it should be a *safe* space, almost a sanctuary, which means it is secure from interruptions. Even a knock on the door is more than a distraction; it is a violation. I always disconnect the telephone and hang a "Do Not Disturb" sign on the door before we begin our work. Then we can pray together or sit in silence, weep or talk, and know that for a little while, for sixty minutes, there will be no intruders and no distractions. Even though the time is limited (and I believe that this limitation should be observed, except under unusual circumstances), there is—paradoxically—the sense of all the time in the world. In the safe space that has been created, the director can be totally committed, attentive only to the welfare of the guest.

The directee should feel unhurried. I find that people often arrive in a state of great distraction, perhaps anxious because the bus was slow or they couldn't find a parking place or perhaps anxious because this meeting feels—somehow—like an appointment to talk with God, and they aren't sure how to begin the conversation. Perhaps this is why my first meeting with Thomas was decidedly uncomfortable. Thomas is a physician, a third-year resident in an inner-city teaching hospital. His hours are long, and his work demanding, surrounded by people in great pain, many of them facing death. God has gotten his attention, and going to church on Sunday isn't enough. A mutual friend told Thomas about me, but in her enthusiasm, she did us both an unwitting disservice by painting a glowing picture of spiritual direction in general and of my gifts in particular. Thomas arrived, definitely wary of the highly touted guru and not at all sure that candor in God-talk was a good idea. It took us several sessions of cautious testing on his part and determined ordinariness on mine before the space, physical and spiritual, felt truly welcoming to him.

*Chapter One*
WELCOMING THE STRANGER

Then, too, the director can unconsciously communicate his own hurriedness and distraction. Even though I try to allow a few minutes to collect myself between appointments or to make the transition from educator-administrator to spiritual director, it doesn't always work. A seminarian arrives to wrestle with issues of vocation, or an incest survivor comes to talk about the difficulty of praying the Our Father while memories of an earthly father-rapist flood her mind, and I am caught up in syllabus preparation or altercations with the Business Office. No matter how inviting the physical space might be, I have inner preparations to make before I can offer true hospitality.

*We Begin in Silence*

It helps to begin with silence. If nothing else, the time with the directee is thereby set aside as a time of prayer, not as a conference or a friendly chat. The length of the silence may vary. In the early stages of working together, the directee may find it unsettling if the stillness goes on too long, but the quiet time can extend as trust grows. Emily and I once sat together for an hour in complete silence. We had worked together long enough to be comfortable with one another, and on that particular day, she was exhausted from work and family pressures. I had invited her to break the silence when she was ready. Minutes passed, and the silence became deeper and deeper, serene but very alive. I was with her, but in no way anxious to "do" anything for her. At the end of the hour we exchanged the peace, knowing that Aelred's "third" had indeed been present in our midst.

This entry into silence need not be abrupt. With directees whom I have not seen for some time, we often spend a minute or two catching up, perhaps getting a cup of tea or coffee, before settling down to work. Then the silence helps define the borders and makes it clear what we are about. During these initial moments of silence, I try not to pay attention to the directee, but rather to get my own house in order. It helps to have an upright posture, hands open and

# HOLY LISTENING
*The Art of Spiritual Direction*

relaxed, and breathing slowed. And then I pray. Sometimes it is the Jesus Prayer--"Lord Jesus Christ, have mercy on me, a sinner"--sometimes short, childish prayers of petition: Dear God, help me pay attention! Dear God, help me keep my mouth shut! Dear God, let me put myself out of the way! Dear God, let me be wholly present to this person, your child!

I have read that physicians can make extensive and accurate diagnoses merely by shaking hands with the patient, and silence shared with the directee is in some ways such a diagnostic instrument. Although we are not clinicians, it can tell us a great deal. With our eyes closed and our hearts centered in prayer, we can pick up fear, anxiety, fatigue, rage, hope, and yearning—the whole spectrum of human feeling.

Sometimes, as with Emily, I ask the directee to end the silence when she is ready. Because people panic if they are asked to pray, I phrase this request in general terms: "Let's be quiet together for a few minutes, and then you begin whenever you are ready." I have learned to say this very clearly and with sufficient volume: prayerful silence is out of the question if either of us is unsure of the ground rules. For those who are uneasy or fearful of not saying "the right thing," responsibility for beginning the conversation can be a burden. Then I end the silence with a prayer. Perhaps the Trisagion (Holy God, holy and mighty, holy immortal One, have mercy upon us), perhaps a simple "Come, Lord Jesus," an invocation of the Holy Spirit, or just "Amen."

I have learned to trust the little prayers that come into my mind, having long ago given up the idea that there is one correct way of gathering the silence together and moving out if it. Now I catch myself wondering what will pop into my head. Not too long ago, I was surprised to hear inwardly a German table blessing that I had learned as a very small child. I resisted it, because we were not sitting at a table and it seemed so inappropriate, But it wouldn't go away, and so I broke the silence with it: "Come, Lord Jesus, and be our guest, and bless everything that you have given us." Only

*Chapter One*
## WELCOMING THE STRANGER

upon reflection did I realize that it was a nearly perfect prayer of hospitality, a prayer about the mysterious reversal of host and guest that lies at the heart of spiritual direction.

*A Safe Place*

The space and time provided for the directee is safe not only because it is free from interruption, but also because *anything* may be said without fear of criticism or exposure. The confidentiality of the spiritual direction session is or should be as inviolable as that of the confessional. It is important to make it clear at the initial, exploratory meeting that you will not discuss with others anything that has been said during your time together. This seal can lead to delicate, even humorous situations within a small community such as the seminary, where most of us wear several hats. The safest path for me has been the cultivation of amnesia, even about "harmless" details, since it is difficult to remember where I first heard bits of news about jobs, pregnancies, crises, and triumphs. Even in a context larger than a parish or a seminary, the spiritual direction community is a surprisingly small one. It is prudent to assume that *everyone* knows each other.

For the same reason, I am reluctant to maintain any kind of written records, although I know that some directors, including such prestigious ones as the late Martin Thornton, advocate some form of record-keeping, as a reminder of relevant issues or as progress notes.[3] In my view, however, this is one of the ways in which spiritual direction should be distinguished from psychotherapy. We must have a discerning eye, but we are not diagnosticians in a clinical sense, for we risk diminishing our spiritual guests if we reduce them to symptoms and measurements. The person sitting opposite me is always a mystery. When I label, I limit.

People's secrets—the secrets of their lives and more especially the secrets of their souls—are precious. We live in a time when most of us can talk easily about sex, somewhat less comfortably about death, and only with the greatest difficulty about our relationship with God. To inquire how people pray is to ask *the* intimate question. I still remember a time in a crowded bookstore when James, a young priest-friend, said quite out of nowhere and in a voice that carried, "You know, Margaret, you've never told me how you pray. What do you do, anyway?" I had a feeling of *deja vu*, carried back to a time at the supermarket checkout when one of my children, in a clarion voice, asked, "But how do the babies get *inside* in the first place?" To James, as with the child at the checkout, I hastily said, "I'll tell you when we get outside."

My approach to talking about prayer is often circumspect. I might begin by asking about the directee's daily rhythms—are there times when she can be alone and quiet? Are there places that seem especially "safe" and close to God? A bit of self-disclosure might help. Carol was reluctant to talk about prayer because she was so anxious and apologetic about praying "enough" and praying "right." One day I commented that while reading the Daily Office sometimes seemed mechanical and dry, however commendable, to me God felt very close and prayer seemed very real in the stillness of the morning, before the alarm clock sounded. Carol said: "I pray the Connecticut Turnpike. I use the toll booths as markers, like the big beads on the rosary." Her entire daily commute was a time of prayer, but she felt that it didn't "count," that she should be doing something more "spiritual," and that her aging Toyota could not qualify as a holy space.

Beyond the predictable difficulty of talking about prayer under any circumstances, people come to us burdened by sin, real and imagined, and by shame. The person recovering from addiction needs to feel safe with us; the survivor of sexual abuse needs to know that no detail can shock or disgust us. The penitent needs to know that we hear but do not judge, that we stand ready to untangle the strands of sin and shame. This total acceptance does not mean that sin is taken lightly or that the consequences of destructive or hurtful behavior are glossed over. "Oh well, never mind," and "You

*Chapter One*
WELCOMING THE STRANGER

did WHAT??!!" are equally wicked and irresponsible reactions to the baring of a soul. The director who is convinced of God's love and mercy, even when the directee is not, is able to accept any disclosure with equanimity. Through her loving acceptance she is able to model and reflect the love of God so yearned for by the directee who despairs of his own worthiness.

A good host gives the guest the sense that there is all the time in the world, even when they both know that time is a precious commodity. Unless I am able to put *everything* aside, I have failed in hospitality. Ordinary business can be banished with relative ease, but it is more difficult to quiet deeper unrest, such as my own anger, fear, or fatigue—all of which have little to do with the person sitting opposite me. If I am to do my work optimally, they must be put aside, at least for the next hour. The gift of hospitality in this time is the gift of myself, which may not be much, but it is all that I have.

As someone who likes to talk and who enjoys human company, one of my hardest lessons in spiritual direction has been that less is frequently more. Unrestrained empathy can lead us to appropriation of the other person's experience, by posture and by facial expression if not by words. I guard myself (not always successfully) by two means. First, I use the Jesus Prayer, my "egg-timer" prayer. When I feel myself crowding someone emotionally or spiritually, I tell myself, "Ten Jesus Prayers before you say anything!" Or when I become impatient that we seem to be getting nowhere, I promise myself, "Five Jesus Prayers, and then you blow the whistle." That simple old prayer has held me back from foolishness and harm more often than I can tell. Second, I pay attention to my hands. Grantly Dick Read, in his seminal book on natural childbirth, stressed the importance of a relaxed face: if the birthgiver was able to relax her facial muscles, she was able to relax totally. I can't watch my own face, but hands are another matter. So long as they are open and receptive in my lap or resting easily on the arms of my

# HOLY LISTENING
*The Art of Spiritual Direction*

chair, I am able to convey a sense of leisure because I myself feel unhurried.

Hospitality must have a beginning and an end; guests cease to be guests if they come to live with us. As director, it is my responsibility to keep track of the time and to draw the meeting to a close at the proper moment. An hour is sufficient; after that, the conversation tends to become repetitive or trivialized. (I make an exception for directees who travel from a considerable distance and whom I see less frequently.) I am greatly helped by a small, retired alarm clock placed unobtrusively behind the visitor's chair, which allows me to note the passage of time without looking at my watch. About ten minutes before the time is up, I manage to interject, "We'll have to stop in a few minutes." These words almost always result in a sharpened focus, and the most important material of the session may be introduced at this point. It is tempting to extend the time when these "doorknob manifestations" occur, but I try to resist the temptation. The directee needs to value our time together and make optimum use of it. So I usually say something like, "That seems significant. Let's start with that next time."

*Listening to the Story*

If spiritual direction is hospitality, offering a place for rest and cleansing, the director's assessment of what is and is not valuable material is at best skewed. Sometimes there is a great deal of garbage to be dumped (to use the trailer park image) or layers of rust to be scoured away, in the housewifely idiom of Catherine of Genoa. This calls for patience and openness. Story-telling needs to be unhurried and unharried, so the listener must be willing to let the narrative unfold, to be sensitive to seeming repetitions—are they plodding in a circle, or do they spiral? Are there gems hidden in the trash? Is the storyteller testing the reliability of the listener, or denying herself the protagonist's role and centering everywhere but on herself? So Mildred wants to talk only about her husband's vocational crisis: what can she do to help him?

*Chapter One*
WELCOMING THE STRANGER

And Jane wants to talk about her rector, for whom she functions as a kind of older sister: how can he be protected from predatory wardens? How can she help him learn to delegate responsibility?

Storytelling is also a dialogue, and sometimes the listener-director must become active in helping shape the story. So I might say to Mildred, "This is your time, not David's. What about you?" And I must be prepared for her response: "I want only what's best for him. I want to help him." She is resistant. I cannot let her go on avoiding her own inner exploration, but neither can I become impatient. She must be willing to focus on herself, not because she fears my displeasure, but because she acknowledges her own worth, or because she knows that nothing in her *own* story, however shameful it might seem, is unsayable here. Jane is easier. A kind woman, who loves to take care of people now that her children have left the nest, she needs only a gentle reminder that her rector can look after himself, and this is the time and place to look after Jane.

At least in the initial stages of the relationship, the story told may seem unimportant, even (as with Mildred) a determined diversion. Understandably so, for this is a time of testing. Tony talks at length about his difficulties at work, where the pressures of office politics make a mockery of his prayer life. What he says is all "true," but I know that we are nowhere near the heart of the matter, although spiralling ever closer. Not long ago he said to me, "I think I trust you. There are more things I want to talk about someday." I have no idea what these "things" might be and feel no particular curiosity about them. As his host, I respect his privacy and say only, "I'm here when you want me. You'll know when the time is right." Trust must be allowed to build. I discover that it forms in strata: just when I think we are hopelessly stuck in banalities or stranded on a plateau, there is a sudden new openness. Or, just when I think that we have "arrived," we move to a new and deeper level.

# HOLY LISTENING
*The Art of Spiritual Direction*

When enough trust has developed so that the directee feels safe to discard these diversions, the work of cleansing begins. Here the director's task is to discern between dirt and disorder, sin and shame. Most of us are well meaning but cluttered, overstimulated, and pulled in a dozen directions at once. Sometimes I wonder if the care of souls was easier in simpler times, for people sometimes come looking for a spiritual director because they are overwhelmed with good things: challenging work, useful charitable activities, more books than they can read and cultural events than they can ever absorb, more information than they can process, more paths of self-improvement than they can follow. Like overindulged children, they are inundated by good things; and they simultaneously yearn and fear to hear: "One thing is needful." They come because they want that one thing, even when they cannot articulate their need. They want help in clearing away the clutter, or at least in arranging it so that it becomes useful spiritual furniture rather than an impediment to wholeness.

*Asking Questions*

Here the director can help by asking the right questions. Simple, direct questions that cut to the heart of the matter are part of the spiritual tradition. Jesus had a way of sweeping distractions out of the way with a trenchant question. To the blind beggar Bartimaeus he asked: "What do you want me to do for you?" To the disciples of John the Baptist, as they crept along behind him, attracted yet cautious: "What do you seek?" To the disciples, despairing of having enough to feed the multitude: "How many loaves have you? Go and see." The four gospels alone provide enough questions for spiritual directors to use in clearing away the clutter and helping the directee articulate a yearning for God.

The question Jesus put to Bartimaeus is an invaluable aid to clarity and order. When posed by the director it may meet with resistance, especially in women, who have been socialized early to want nothing (at least overtly!) and to put their

*Chapter One*
WELCOMING THE STRANGER

own needs aside in the service and care of others. This is a time to be gently persistent. "What do you want me—as director—to do for you? And what do you want Christ do for you?" To get at the answer is not unlike peeling an onion, having first persuaded the directee that it is "all right" to want something, that a God who invites us to say "Abba" must expect childlike (if not childish) behavior from us.

Directees who are the victims of niceness need to be reminded that such niceness, however costly and painfully achieved, is not one of the cardinal virtues. They are often surprised when I refer them to scriptural precedents for persistence, even nagging, in their prayers of petition. Even those who claim moderate acquaintance with the Bible forget about the Canaanite woman, who simply would not stop asking for Jesus' help, even though he tried to dismiss her with an abruptness that would earn him a failing mark in pastoral presence:

> ...She came and knelt before him, saying "Lord, help me." He answered, "It is not fair to take the children's food and throw it to the dogs." She said, "Yes, Lord, yet even the dogs eat the crumbs that fall from their masters' table." Then Jesus answered her, "Woman, great is your faith! Let it done for you as you wish." And her daughter was healed instantly (Matt. 15:25-28).

This is a shocking story for those who believe that prayer must be polite to the point of diffidence. Even more shocking are the parables recorded by Luke, stories that seem to encourage bad manners, even obnoxious behavior in prayer. Directees who are fearful of testing God's patience to the breaking point can be helped by Luke's ironic overstatement in the story of the dishonest judge and the persistent widow. Like the outcast Canaanite woman who refuses to leave Jesus alone until her daughter is healed, the widow does not let go lightly. Finally the judge gives in:

> For a while he refused; but later he said to himself, "Though I have no fear of God and no respect for anyone, yet because this widow keeps bothering me, I will grant

her justice, so that she may not wear me out by continually coming" (Lk. 18:4-5).

To be able to say what one truly wants or where one is in pain is a great step toward achieving order in one's spiritual household. People come to direction wanting and needing many things but—unlike the troublesome widow—fearful of "bothering" God and unaware of God's invitation to do just that! Further, they come to us unsure of their priorities; in the material and emotional overabundance of our culture, they have been stimulated to love and want many things. They come in the disarray of their disordered loves, not knowing or perhaps only sensing their need to strip away the layers and articulate what they really want: God. In a way, spiritual direction is a protracted discussion of the two Great Commandments:

> 'You shall love the Lord your God with all your heart, and with all your soul, and with all your mind.' This is the greatest and first commandment. And a second is like it: 'You shall love your neighbor as yourself.' On these two commandments hang all the law and the prophets (Matt. 22:37-40).

When all the layers have been stripped away, God is what the directee wants. There may be other legitimate, laudable wants—physical and mental health, meaningful work, sound and stable relationships—as well as other, less laudable loves and desires masked as pious yearnings—the desire to manipulate and control, the avoidance of responsible engagement, spiritual posturing rooted in a catalytic mixture of pride and self-hatred—to name just a few.

*Taking Out the Garbage*

When I was a student in Switzerland, decades ago, bathing was not to be taken lightly: the water had to be heated, and sometimes the landlady charged extra for the use of fuel. In the house where I lived, the privilege was free, but the bathtub was in an unheated, outdoor cellar. So when I visited friends who lived in a modern apartment with unlimited hot

*Chapter One*
## WELCOMING THE STRANGER

water, there was no question of how they might best entertain me—they retired early, leaving me to splash and soak. Now I enjoy repaying the debt of their hospitality: some of my favorite houseguests in New York are young people who travel with backpacks and are used to the minimal comfort of hostels and dormitories. After I have fed them heartily, I retire early and leave them to enjoy the hot shower and the washing machine.

Order is not synonymous with cleanliness. People come to direction burdened with a sense of their own unworthiness and unloveliness, crushing shame, and their own sins. What a tangle! As the story is told, it is the director's task gently to pick apart the strands, never to minimize the directee's pain or responsibility for her own actions—and then to deal with the garbage. There is the shame of the recovering addict, the lingering sense of uncleanness that haunts the incest survivor, the painful memory of an abortion, the anguish of broken relationships that can never be restored, the burden of trespasses long forgotten by all save the trespasser. There is great variety in the garbage. It may contain hidden treasures and nearly always provides a fertile medium for growth, even when it is unlovely and smells bad.

Those who come to spiritual direction burdened with their sinfulness come in need of cleansing and healing. Julian of Norwich likens the errant soul to a headstrong toddler who must be free to run and explore her little world if she is to grow to maturity, but who inevitably falls, tearing her clothing and becoming hurt and dirty. This is a homely and engaging picture of the sinner, crying out—as Julian puts it—not to a God of punishment but to a loving mother Christ. The loving mother picks up the toddler, cleans and comforts it, then holds it close. As we listen to the stories of our guests, again and again we hear them say the twentieth-century equivalent of Julian's words: "My kind mother, my gracious mother, my beloved mother, have mercy on me. I have made myself filthy and unlike you, and I may not and cannot make it right without your grace and help."[4]

# HOLY LISTENING
*The Art of Spiritual Direction*

I am struck by the overlapping of spiritual direction and sacramental confession. In both it is essential that the story be told candidly, that sins and shortcomings be named, that the directee see himself clearly. St. Anthony in the desert knew the importance of recognizing and naming the demons. Exposure is salutary. My grandmother, living before the time of antibiotics and practicing the folk medicine inherited from her rural foremothers, knew that healing was promoted by cleansing, then by exposure to light and air. As spiritual directors, whether lay or ordained, we are purveyors of light and air. We hear confessions, stories of hurt received and hurt inflicted, of shabbiness and coldness of heart, of myriad little murders. Some of our directees might shrink if we began the session by inviting them to make a formal sacramental confession, but if we let them know that we sense their burden and gently invite them to speak of it, the sense of relief is almost palpable. Others, who are at ease with the sacrament of reconciliation, may use spiritual direction as a means of preparing for confession; or, if the director is also the confessor, regular celebration of the sacrament can be woven into the fabric of the relationship.

The *Parzival* of Wolfram von Eschenbach is a parable of that kind of hospitality. The foolish knight has travelled and quested for years, unwittingly leaving hurt and destruction in his wake—he has left his mother to die of loneliness and a broken heart, he has killed his (unrecognized) cousin and then despoiled the corpse, he has brought degradation and suffering to a married woman whose husband did not understand his clumsy and asexual embraces of her. Most seriously, he has let social convention stand in the way of true compassion, for when he saw the excruciating suffering of the Grail King, his mistaken understanding of chivalric behavior prevented his asking the saving question: "What's wrong? What hurts?"

On Good Friday, chance or grace brings him to the hermit Trevrizent. What occurs between them is a model of hospitality and a model of spiritual direction, particularly in

*Chapter One*
WELCOMING THE STRANGER

its purgative and healing aspects. The old man knows that the youth is burdened with anger and guilt, that he lacks self-understanding, and that he is spiritually as well as physically lost in a trackless wasteland. But like a good director, he is patient--helping Parzival feed and stable his horse, inviting the young man to warm himself by the meager fire, sharing his simple food.

Finally Parzival tells his story, or rather, he makes his confession, for his story is one long account of wandering far from God. Trevrizent hears it gravely, without minimizing or dismissing anything. Then, in a kind of absolution, he tells Parzival: "Give your sins to me. In the sight of God, I am guaranty for your atonement." Sitting in his cold cave in a Germanic forest, he is a northern echo of Abba Lot, austere father of the Egyptian desert, who said to his troubled penitent, "Confess it to me, and I will carry it."[5]

This is perhaps the ultimate act of hospitality, epitomizing the generous mutuality of the direction relationship. Like Abba Bessarion, the director knows that he, too, is a sinner: "A brother who had sinned was turned out of his church by the priest; Abba Bessarion got up and went to him, saying, 'I, too, am a sinner.'"[6] Director and directee are united in the glory and sinfulness of their humanity; they are part of the same family.

When we listen compassionately with "the mind in the heart," as Theophan the Recluse puts it, we cannot help taking others' sins upon ourselves. After a day of listening, I often feel heavy and tired, with queasy stomach and aching head. It helped me to understand my somatic reactions when I remembered novelist-theologian Charles Williams and his theory of "exchange" and "substituted love." He took very seriously the exhortation in Paul's letter to the Galatians that we "bear one another's burdens and so fulfil the law of Christ," and might have been thinking of uneasy spiritual directors when he wrote:

> St. Paul's injunction is to such acts as 'fulfil the law of Christ', that is, to acts of substitution. To take over the grief

> or the fear or the anxiety of another is precisely that; and precisely that is less practised than praised....
>
> The one who gives has to remember that he has parted with his burden, that it is being carried by another, that his part is to believe that and be at peace....The one who takes has to set himself—mind and emotion and sensation—to the burden, to know it, imagine it, receive it—and sometimes not to be taken aback by the swiftness of the divine grace and the lightness of the burden.[7]

I am still learning my obligations in the contract, and perhaps I am slow to let go. Yet I cannot believe that it is so effortless as Williams suggests. Unless I experience some heaviness, how do I know I have accepted a burden? There is a cheapness and spiritual dishonesty in opening oneself to another's story while keeping one's fingers crossed—"I'll let it touch me, even touch me deeply, but not for long." On the other hand, I accept the burden, not to hoard and cherish it as mine but rather to pass it on immediately. As Williams observes, "the carrying of the cross may be light because it is not to the crucifixion."[8]

In our culture it often seems a mark of professionalism to be impervious to others' pain. Sometimes this is a good thing: I would prefer that my surgeon operate with eyes not blurred with tears! Yet in some areas we have gone too far, and, along with their own woundedness, our healers deny the reality of others' suffering. Spiritual directors are not professionals, but amateurs who aspire to reflect Christ's love. So we take sin and pain upon ourselves, not in grandiose self-promotion, but because the assumption of such a burden is one of the risks of hospitality.

Yet we don't have to keep that burden, dragging ever-heavier loads of pain and sin, because we can let it go in our prayers—both for ourselves and for our directees. We can let it go in holy forgetting, remembering that God was managing nicely before we joined the firm and will continue to cope after we have returned to dust. We can let it go by all our devices for refreshment and self-restoration. But first of all,

*Chapter One*
WELCOMING THE STRANGER

*we must let ourselves be touched.* Trevrizent's hospitality was not cheap, even though the accommodations were minimal and the food a handful of herbs.

As spiritual directors, we have the authority to assure our directees of God's love and forgiveness, and those of us who are ordained can declare absolution. While I like to know what I'm doing and therefore prefer to keep spiritual direction and sacramental confession distinct, there are times when I can say, "What you have just told me is a confession. I am convinced that you are deeply sorry for these things in your past, indeed contrite. So I would like to offer you absolution." For those to whom this is alien, even a little frightening, some brief teaching is in order. Then, as we end our meeting with absolution and a blessing, I can almost feel the heaviness drop from the directee.

Sometimes it is better to suggest that the directee consider making a formal confession in the near future. On one occasion, a woman sought me out to tell me about her abortion, performed decades ago when she was very young. At the time, it seemed her only course, but she had never ceased to mourn secretly for her unborn child. She seemed surprised when I spoke of her obvious love for her baby; she had seen only her guilt, not the love entangled in it. The woman was not accustomed to making her confession, so I suggested she look at the rite of reconciliation in the Book of Common Prayer, particularly at the second form. Then, if it seemed right to her, we would celebrate the sacrament together that evening. We did, and I have never felt so sure that there was rejoicing in heaven as we embraced and I told her to go in peace, that the Lord had put away all her sins.

Lay directors and those from traditions lacking the sacrament of reconciliation need to remember that all baptized persons can declare God's forgiveness to those who are truly contrite. In my hospital ministry, before I was ordained, I once visited a woman scheduled for major surgery the next morning. She told me that she was Roman Catholic, but that she had not made her confession in a very long time. When I offered to call the Roman Catholic chaplain, she responded with mingled panic and despair. "No, no, it's too late!" We sat together for a while and then I said, "But you want to tell God that you are sorry?" She didn't say anything, but fell into my arms and wept. After a moment, I assured her of God's forgiveness. We exchanged the peace, and I wished her a good night.

*Sharing the Story*

For me, spiritual direction is *always* storytelling. I don't mean that we move doggedly through the directee's life, year by year and decade by decade. The story moves around in time, gliding or leaping from present to past, from present to future. Without the story, there is no flesh, no blood, no specificity. But I find that it doesn't matter where we begin. It is always a story of a journey, always a story about relationship with God—whether the directee is fleeing the Hound of Heaven, or lost, or yearning, or living among the swine and eating their husks.

The director's task is to help connect the individual's story to *the* story and thereby help the directee to recognize and claim identity in Christ, discern the action of the Holy Spirit. There is a God-component in all human experience, even in lives that seem pain-filled and remote from God. A sense of God's absence or remorse at one's own inattentiveness to God's presence can be a fruitful place for beginning direction. However the story is structured, it eventually includes fragments of the story from the past, the present, and the future.

Even when someone's earlier life has not been marked by extraordinary suffering and pathology, the story of beginnings is important if we are to have a sense of the whole person. Birth order, ethnicity, and remembered familial warmth (or lack of it) all contribute color and form to the picture. I always like to explore people's earliest awareness of God, which is often quite distinct from their family's degree of

*Chapter One*
WELCOMING THE STRANGER

religious observance. For many, spiritual direction is the first opportunity to put this experience into words.

As for the story of the present, it is absurd to talk about "prayer" as an abstraction; it must always be connected with the directee's "real" life. This does not mean that there is no talk of prayer as such, for people come to us seeking practical help in finding the rhythms and forms of prayer that are most fruitful for them. But I am nervous of those who want to talk *only* of prayer, and in those cases I feel free to ask questions: tell me about your work, your family, your friends, your health. Where is your Christian community? What do you do for fun? Again and again, I discover that deep concerns have been pushed aside as not sufficiently lofty to discuss in this setting. A deteriorating marriage, an adolescent son caught in addiction, or daily work that deadens the soul are all spiritual issues and, as such, a crucial part of the story.

This story must reach into the future. Spiritual direction is about hope, and there is always a next step. One of my most helpful mentors in helping directees discern this next step is Mr. Dick, Aunt Betsey's eccentric lodger in Charles Dickens' *David Copperfield*. Nowadays he would be classified as "developmentally impaired," but Dickens presents him as childlike, loving, and firmly grounded in reality. Repeatedly, Aunt Betsey turns to Mr. Dick for counsel in complicated situations; his advice is always compassionate and eminently practical, going right to the heart of the matter. Confronted with a dirty, hungry, exhausted runaway child, he is cheerfully unaware of legal and familial complexities.

> "Well, then," returned my aunt.... "Here you see young David Copperfield, and the question I put to you is, what shall I do with him?"
>
> "What shall you do with him?" said Mr. Dick feebly, scratching his head. "Oh! do with him?"
>
> "Yes," said my aunt with a grave look, and her forefinger held up. "Come! I want some very sound advice."

33

> "Why, if I was you," said Mr. Dick, considering, and looking vacantly at me, "I should—" The contemplation of me seemed to inspire him with a sudden idea, and he added briskly, "I should wash him!"[9]

Similarly, when the child becomes a permanent member of this unlikely household, Mr. Dick does not borrow trouble by speculating about possible courses of action far in the future, but suggests with great practicality, "Have him measured for a suit of clothes directly." Our directees rarely need to be provided with literal scrubbing or garments, but their next steps, to be taken in hope, are often as small and simple as those offered by Mr. Dick. The journey is not to be completed in a day, and the path leading to its end is twisted and invisible, but we can help them see the next small, often deceptively simple steps.

If spiritual direction is about hope, it is also about death. When I left secular teaching to pursue ordination to the priesthood, I felt called to work with the dying. Practical experience in the hospital and with the frail aged in a nursing home confirmed my gifts in this ministry. While it was emotionally and spiritually taxing, it was also fulfilling beyond all my expectations. It must be a sign of God's gracious (and ironic) humor that I no longer walk dark and empty corridors in the middle of the night or watch physical strength diminish and once-clear minds grow dim with age. At first I was disappointed to exchange work at life's thresholds for this quiet, well-groomed business of sitting and listening, until I realized I was still working with the dying. It is no longer fashionable to talk about preparing for a "good death," yet that is what spiritual direction is all about. The journey does have an end, and our physical death is one of its markers. Even when it is not clearly articulated, people come to spiritual direction grappling with questions of their own mortality. We can help in this as we explore the story of the future.

*Chapter One*
WELCOMING THE STRANGER

*Self-Disclosure*

Storytelling, as I have noted, is not a solitary activity: directors are primarily listeners, but also participants in their own right. Sometimes this participation appears passive, consisting chiefly of keeping quiet and staying out of the way, attentive but not overpowering, but directors should not fear the self-revelation that comes from joining the conversation. It may be no more than acknowledging their own difficulties in faithfulness at prayer or the all-too-human flaw of unreal expectations. Directees tend to set extremely high standards for themselves and expect, in their new state of self-awareness, that they will not become impatient or succumb to petty maliciousness. A director's shared humanity can be a valuable corrective.

This willingness toward self-disclosure is one of the primary distinctions between spiritual direction and psychotherapy, where the mutuality of the former is an essential characteristic of the relationship. The director should always be aware that she too is a traveler, neither an authority nor a guru. Thoughtful self-disclosure is one way of remaining grounded and human, although it must be intentional and judicious, else the direction session will degenerate into a cozy chat. So I ask myself: "Why am I doing this? Will it help the directee? Or will my self-revelation be harmful, appropriating time, attention, and energy that rightly belong to the person sitting opposite me?"

Most of my directees know that I am married and that I have reared children, but I try to avoid the exchange of friendly family anecdotes. They all know that I am a priest. They can figure out my age approximately by looking at me or precisely by consulting the Clerical Directory. Occasionally, they will want to know more, and there are points at which hearing some of the director's story is an encouragement, a reassurance and reminder that we are travelling the same road. So in initial meetings, I make it a practice to ask if there is anything about me the directee would like to know. The most common questions at this point are, "What brought you here? How did you start doing this work?" As the relationship develops and a level of mutual comfort has been established, the directee is usually able to take the initiative in asking questions, such as "Did you ever feel this way? Did this ever happen to you?" Tacitly I have given permission to be challenged and probed to the degree that such sharing of experience is helpful to the directee. It is a delicate and dangerous business, for I can use the directee to feed my ego. For example, I have to be especially careful with Jo, who is eager to attribute to me wisdom and compassion beyond my most extravagant dreams. But I know that I am in danger of seduction, however loving and unwitting its intent; and so I resist her invitation to talk very much about myself.

However I join in the storytelling, whether by invitation or my own intuition, our sense of solidarity is increased. We are united in our sinfulness, our baptism, and the commonalities of our journeys. I need not say much, just a few words to help make the connections. Thus to Penny, mother of a troubled and troubling teenage, I remarked: "Being a mother can be heartbreaking work. Everyone who's been there has at least some idea of what you're going through." Penny didn't need to hear details of my life as mother of (now happily grownup) adolescents, but it helped her to know that we shared this particular experience.

Careful self-revelation by the director is also valuable in dealing with projection and transference. Like all human beings, directees see what they want to see and hence attribute to us impossible degrees of holiness and wisdom. Like Jo, who would rather hear about me than talk about herself, they are unwilling to let us be ourselves—mere human beings capable of sin and shabbiness. Instead, they are willing, indeed eager, to elevate us to great heights of wisdom and sanctity; we can buy into this spiritual inflation or apply a needed corrective. Particularly in the early stages of the relationship, especially with those to whom the whole idea of spiritual direction is new, we run the risk of being put on a pedestal. We can defuse this by what we choose to reveal

*Chapter One*
WELCOMING THE STRANGER

about ourselves—our own falling short in prayer; our tendency toward sloth, impatience, or greed; our times of aridity. By no means do we turn the relationship around and overwhelm the directee with our own shortcomings, but carefully and lightly try to communicate that we have neither magic powers nor a direct line to God's ear. We are only fellow travelers—at different places on the road, perhaps, but fallible and ordinary nonetheless.

We reveal ourselves in more than words. Anyone coming into my office knows that I love icon reproductions, that my bookshelf is eclectic, that I support the ordination of women to the episcopate (a regal purple teatowel, given to me by English friends and tacked on the inside of the door, proclaims this), and that I like rocks from my beloved Virginia river and fresh flowers from the corner greengrocer. We also reveal ourselves also in what we wear. This is more of an issue for directors who are clergy or members of religious orders, for a black shirt and stiff white collar or a habit carries a powerful message of authority and hierarchy. Sometimes this is helpful: directees want to be sure that they are entrusting themselves to someone competent, and clerical garb may be reassuring. It also depersonalizes the situation, in that we present ourselves as "priest" or "religious" and not as "man" or "woman." This can backfire, however, when—as frequently and quite healthily occurs—the directee confuses intimacy with God with human intimacy. Add to this romanticized projections about God-people in costume, and clerical or religious dress becomes an impediment.

So I am careful about what I wear. Some people are most comfortable talking with a clearly labelled priest, particularly when they are still testing the waters of our relationship or dealing with painful or shame-filled material. Others are over-impressed by externals and have difficulty getting down to reality. If the director is in full costume, they seem to think, it is proper to talk only about prayer in the narrowest sense and to avoid any faintly "improper" language or emotions. So it helps to turn up at least part of the time in an un-

# HOLY LISTENING
*The Art of Spiritual Direction*

remarkable dress or suit; I haven't gone so far as blue jeans and a sweatshirt, but I can imagine situations in which such informality would be liberating.

I am constantly surprised at how much shared laughter there is in spiritual direction. At first, I was sure that I was doing something wrong; after all, spiritual direction is serious business, and surely laughter has no place in it. But again and again, I find myself laughing *with* directees, never *at* them. What a pity there is no reference in the gospels to our Lord's laughter! Gentle, nonintrusive humor has a way of restoring perspective, or reducing our inflated selves to manageable proportions. Laughter makes and keeps us childlike.

We also share tears. I do not cry easily, especially in the presence of others, but there are times in spiritual direction when words are out of place and, to my initial dismay, I feel tears flooding my eyes. This happened in my work with Linda, a survivor of years of incestuous abuse. More than once, as she shared the details of her unimaginable pain and degradation, I was left without words. There *were* no words that were not cheap, that did not somehow dishonor her experience. For a while, I tried to deal with my tears surreptitiously; after all, it didn't seem like professional behavior! So I would prop my chin on my hand, in a posture of intense listening and then make what I thought were unobtrusive swipes at the tears.

Years have passed, and now Linda has reached a place of grace and hope. Not long ago she said to me, "I can't tell you how much it meant to me the times you cried with me." So much for my studiedly casual whisking away of my tears! By no means do I recommend weeping as a device, nor do I suggest that directors train themselves to cry on cue. But the importance of shared emotion, of empathy and compassion cannot be underestimated.

The fact of being entrusted with someone's soul, of being allowed to enter the story, however layered and convoluted it might be, is staggering. Fortunately, there is yet another

*Chapter One*
WELCOMING THE STRANGER

surprise in store for the spiritual director. Like Sarah baking the cakes or the unnamed servant dressing the calf, the director is a necessary, but distinctly secondary figure in the offering of hospitality. Without warning, the role of host, of Guest Giver, is preempted! This should not be surprising, for the gospels offer precedents: Jesus had a way of taking over at the dinner table. So too in the ministry of spiritual direction—when all is said and done, the Holy Spirit is the true director. I find this reassuring when I am overcome by performance anxiety. Will I be wise? Will I be sufficiently holy, or at least look that way? Will I do even a half-way decent job? But if I am ready to relinquish my role to the true Host, the burden of responsibility drops away and the space I have prepared becomes gracious and holy.

# Endnotes

1  Ward, *Desert Christian*, p. 104.

2  Aelred of Rievaulx, *Spiritual Friendship* (Kalamazoo, MI: Cistercian Publications, 1977), pp. 71-72.

3  Martin Thornton, *Spiritual Direction* (Cambridge, MA: Cowley, 1984), p. 127.

4  Julian of Norwich, *Showings* (New York: Paulist, 1978), p. 301.

5  Wolfram von Eschenbach, *Parzival*, trans. Helen M. Mustard and Charles E. Passage (New York: Vintage, 1961), p. 268; Ward, *Desert Christian*, p. 122.

6  *Ibid.*

7  Charles Williams, *He Came Down From Heaven* (London: William Heinemann, 1938), pp. 123, 125.

8  *Ibid.*, p. 124.

9  Charles Dickens, *David Copperfield* (London: Thomas Nelson and Sons, n.d.), p. 203.

CHAPTER TWO

# Good Teachers

As he was setting out on a journey, a man ran up and knelt before him, and asked him, "Good Teacher, what must I do to inherit eternal life?" Jesus said to him, "Why do you call me good? No one is good but God alone. You know the commandments: 'You shall not murder; You shall not commit adultery; You shall not steal; You shall not bear false witness; You shall not defraud; Honor your father and mother.'" He said to him, "Teacher, I have kept all these since my youth." And Jesus, looking at him, loved him and said, "You lack one thing; go, sell what you own, and give the money to the poor, and you will have treasure in heaven; then come, follow me." When he heard this he was shocked and went away grieving; for he had many possessions.

*Mark 10:17-22*

# Good Teachers

Every now and then I will ride with a member of that vanishing breed of New Yorker philosopher cab-driver, streetwise men with gifts of discernment, who will ask me, "You're a teacher, right, lady?" And I have to say, "Yes, I am," while wondering what gave me away. I am a lot of other things—priest, wife, mother, administrator, lay medical practitioner, scrubber of floors, washer of clothes—but my teacher identity is one that has been with me for nearly as long as I can remember, and it is a true identity, inextricably linked with my priestly one.

I was about six when the pedagogical urge overcame me. I had just learned to read and couldn't wait to impart my newfound skills to my best friend, Peggy, who was two years younger and considerably smaller than I. So we "played school" interminably. Things haven't changed much—the excitement of sharing what has been learned, of mutual exploration and discovery, has remained with me—but what *has* changed is that I am no longer authoritarian. While most of my professional life has been spent in the college classroom, my experience has been varied—I have been teacher of English to foreign students, of humanities to over-indulged, neglected teenagers in a fashionable prep school, and of English literature to pregnant high school girls back in the days when they sought refuge in Florence Crittenton Homes. (We all wept when David Coppperfield was orphaned.) Finally, I taught a night course in technical German for a roomful of electrical engineers, with a few chemists thrown in, which was an exercise in mutual support if ever there was one.

*Chapter Two*
GOOD TEACHERS

When I began the process of ordination to the priesthood, I thought I was shedding the skin of my teacher-identity and "giving up" a life I had loved. As a priest, I envisioned myself working in a parish or possibly in a chaplaincy; ironically, I find myself back in the classroom and rejoice to be there. All the past experience has contributed to my present work and ministry, and I am surrounded by a cloud of witnesses—Peggy sitting patiently on the lowest porch step while I drilled her on the three-tables, the polite Japanese businessmen to whom I tried to demonstrate the difference between "L" and "R," and all those classrooms of German students who couldn't quite catch my enthusiasm for adjective endings or the difference between dative and accusative. I realize that, at least in part, I am a priest because I am a teacher, that my years as a teacher were years of preparation, and that nothing has been wasted or lost.

I still spend considerable time in classrooms, while syllabi and reading lists still claim at least some of my attention. Increasingly, however, I am aware that I am most fully a teacher when I meet with someone for spiritual direction. Increasingly, too, I am aware that what I teach cannot be neatly stated in catalogue course descriptions and that my work is infinitely more complex and subtle than the mere imparting of information. It is true that people will occasionally seek spiritual direction when they might more suitably attend an inquirers' class or read a theological textbook, and I can state without apology that intellectual curiosity about the faith is better satisfied elsewhere. Nor do I teach methods of prayer, even though I stand ready to help directees find the ways and rhythms that are most fruitful for them.

So what does the spiritual director teach? In the simplest and also most profound terms, the spiritual director is simultaneously a learner and a teacher of discernment. What is happening? Where is God in this person's life? What is the story? Where does this person's story fit in our common Christian story? How is the Holy Spirit at work in this person's life? What is missing?

# HOLY LISTENING
*The Art of Spiritual Direction*

The first step in discernment is perception. The director is deeply attentive to the person sitting across the holy space, open and permeable to all that is said and unsaid, revealed and hidden. More importantly, by example and by judicious interpretation, she helps the directee toward equal openness and attentiveness. Together they look, listen, and wait. The work of perception is not easy or automatic: we usually see what we want to see or expect to see. When we seek to discern the action of the Holy Spirit in our lives, we expect the dramatic, even the spectacular. In this we resemble Naaman the leper, a powerful general who traveled from Syria to seek healing from the prophet Elisha. Elisha did not meet him in person, but sent a messenger to tell him to wash himself in the River Jordan. Outraged at the matter-of-fact simplicity of the proposed treatment, Naaman exclaimed:

> Behold, I thought that for me he would surely come out, and stand, and call on the name of the Lord his God, and would wave his hand over the spot, and cure the leprosy! Are not Abana and Pharpar, the rivers of Damascus, better than all the waters of Israel? Could I not wash in them, and be clean? (2 Kg. 5:11-12)

Similarly, a directee may be quick to reject the homely, the ordinary, and the near at hand. Here the director can serve as a guide and teacher, gently pointing out the signs that are at once hidden and obvious.

The second step in the work of discernment is judgment: what does one do with the perception? What are the next steps in dealing with the insight that has come? It is important to focus on the *next* steps, despite the temptation to operate on a grander scale. It is human to want to wait for optimum conditions: I'll begin to pray again in Lent or after I have written this exam or maybe when I have fully recovered from this cold. I'll put my spiritual house in order as soon as things get straightened out at the office. I'll think about God again as soon as the baby sleeps through the night or goes to kindergarten or gets his driver's license. One of the major teachings the director can offer—and offer again and again—

*Chapter Two*
GOOD TEACHERS

is the value of the present moment. The fruits of discernment may be enjoyed far into the future, but the material of perception and the attendant judgment are to be found in the here and now, in the everydayness of the directee's life.

The director's task is two-fold: he must himself be capable of discernment, able to put himself out of the way and be fully present to the person sitting opposite him. At the same time, by encouragement and example, he helps the directee to develop and trust her own powers of discernment. This means that she must be able to look at herself, abandon her defenses, and face into hard questions. It may be more comfortable and considerably easier to be ignorant of what the Holy Spirit is up to.

In *To Know as We Are Known: The Spirituality of Education*, Parker Palmer is actually writing about education, but much of what he says applies to the spiritual direction relationship. Taking his text from 1 Corinthians 13:12—"For now we see in a mirror, dimly, but then we will see face to face. Now I know only in part; then I will know fully, even as I have been fully known"—Palmer is primarily concerned with overcoming the gap between subject and object, the knower and the known. He notes the etymological connection between *truth* and *troth*, and states,

> To know something or someone in truth is to enter troth with the known, to rejoin with new knowing what our minds have put asunder. To know in truth is to become betrothed, to engage the known with one's whole self, an engagement one enters with attentiveness, care, and good will. To know in truth is to allow one's self to be known as well, to be vulnerable to the challenges and changes any true relationship brings. To know in truth is to enter into the life of that which we know and to allow it to enter into ours. Truthful knowing weds the knower and the known; even in separation, the two become part of each other's life and fate.[1]

To know in truth, then, is to allow one's self to be known. This is the truth that became incarnate in Jesus Christ, a truth

# HOLY LISTENING
*The Art of Spiritual Direction*

known not in abstraction, but in relationship. The shared commitment to truth ensures that the spiritual direction relationship is one of true mutuality, for both director and directee must allow themselves to be known. This marks one of the major differences between spiritual direction and psychotherapy: the director must be willing to be known—not just by her credentials, affiliations, and titles, but known in her vulnerability and limitations as a child of God.

Similarly, the directee must be willing to be known, to lay aside his masks one by one, no matter how beautiful and useful. Despite all good intentions, this is not easy work. Spiritual direction attracts a disproportionate number of introverts, who require a great deal of time and patience to reach the level of trust necessary for self-revelation. A friend once likened working with them to coaxing a deer out of the forest: you watch it peering out between the trees, occasionally venturing into the meadow, but a sudden move on your part can send it dashing back into the woods. Yet only by letting ourselves be known to each other and to our deepest selves can we have the assurance that we are known by God. If this inner work is done in spiritual direction, it will have an effect on the relation of the individual to the rest of creation. When he allows himself to be known to himself, to another, and to God, the directee will be aware of the web of relationships that connects him to all creation.

## The Great Model: Jesus the Teacher

The great model for all teachers, and certainly for all teachers who are spiritual directors, is Jesus himself. In the four gospels there are over forty references to him as teacher, and just skimming through them is an enlightening exercise. We learn that he taught "as one having authority" (Matt. 7:29; Mk. 1:22). We know that sometimes his teachings were painful, scarcely to be received by his hearers as good news—"Then he began to teach them that the Son of Man must undergo great suffering, and be rejected....and be killed, and after three days rise again" (Mk. 8:31). Note the

*Chapter Two*
GOOD TEACHERS

rhythm of his teaching: Jesus taught in the "correct" and predictable places, such as the temple and the synagogue, but he also taught at the dinner table and as he walked along the road. His methods were varied—stories, parables, hard questions, koan-like sayings, and authoritative pronouncements—and he also used visual aids. When the Pharisees sought to entrap Jesus in a discussion about the lawfulness of paying taxes to Caesar, he asked them to show him a coin.

> And they brought him a denarius. Then he said to them, "Whose head is this, and whose title?" They said, "The emperor's." Then he said to them, "Give therefore to the emperor the things that are the emperor's, and to God the things that are God's" (Matt. 22:19-21).

The simplicity and concreteness of his response cut through all entanglements. When his questioners heard it, they "marveled" and departed.

Jesus taught also by indirection and silence, most notably in the story of the woman taken in adultery, when his studied inattention must have infuriated those who wished to catch him in theological or legal error:

> The scribes and the Pharisees brought a woman who had been caught in adultery; and making her stand before all of them, they said to him, "Teacher, this woman was caught in the very act of committing adultery. Now in the law Moses commanded us to stone such women. What do you say?"...Jesus bent down and wrote with his finger on the ground. When they kept on questioning him, he straightened up and said to them, "Let anyone who is without sin among you be the first to throw a stone at her." And once more he bent down and wrote with his finger on the ground. But when they heard it, they went away, one by one (Jn. 8:3-9).

Current jargon would say that he refused to "get hooked." Certainly by his silence Jesus forced his questioners to stop playing games, to abandon both legal quibbles and the urge to violence, and to look within themselves.

# HOLY LISTENING
*The Art of Spiritual Direction*

From the gospels we learn that teaching is a dangerous activity: while Pilate finds no crime in Jesus, his accusers "were insistent, and said, 'He stirs up the people by teaching throughout all Judea, from Galilee where he began even to this place'" (Lk. 23:4-5). Jesus' teaching is clearly subversive, as all transformative work is; it is a good point to be borne in mind by all who undertake the risky business of spiritual direction.

When Jesus is called "teacher" by those especially close to him, there is a special flavor of mingled intimacy and deference in the address. So in Luke's account of his anointing by "the woman of the city, who was a sinner," he recognizes the unspoken criticism in the mind of his host and says, "Simon, I have something to say to you." When the Pharisee answers, "What is it, Teacher?" Jesus responds by citing a hypothetical case, drawn from the world of commerce and hence far removed from the emotion-laden and sensuous scene before them. He invites Simon, a practical man, to solve a problem:

> "A certain creditor had two debtors; one owed five hundred denarii, and the other fifty. When they could not pay, he canceled the debts for both of them. Now which of them will love him more?" Simon answered, "I suppose the one for whom he canceled the greater debt." And Jesus said to him, "You have judged rightly" (Lk. 7:41-43).

At first glance, it appears that Jesus is teaching his host about the woman—her right to be present, to approach Jesus, to receive forgiveness—but then he shifts the focus to Simon.

> Do you see this woman? I entered your house; you gave me no water for my feet, but she has bathed my feet with her tears and dried them with her hair. You gave me no kiss, but from the time I came in she has not stopped kissing my feet. You did not anoint my head with oil, but she has anointed my feet with ointment. Therefore, I tell you, her sins, which were many, have been forgiven; hence she has shown great love. But the one to whom little is forgiven, loves little ( vv. 44-47).

*Chapter Two*
GOOD TEACHERS

When Jesus asks, "Do you see this woman?" it is really a command: "Look at yourself." This is indeed a story of spiritual direction, with the relationship clearly defined. Simon, the powerful and wealthy host, expects to hear truth from his teacher, and Jesus' reproach blends toughness with affection.

As spiritual directors we still encounter Simon's descendants. They are people of good taste who play by the rules. In their way, like Simon, they are generous and open to God. (The Pharisee, after all, invited Jesus to eat with him.) But also like Simon, they cannot believe that God could be guilty of bad taste or poor judgment. With Simon, they think, "If this man were a prophet, he would have known who and what sort of woman this is who is touching him, for she is a sinner." As a good teacher, Jesus leads him to discernment, to a clear understanding of his own perceptions and skewed judgments.

We have another glimpse of Jesus as teacher in his relationship with Mary of Bethany. In Luke's account (10:38-41), she sits at his feet and listens to his teaching. This is not a position of subservience, but rather the posture of the pupil or disciple. Much is left unsaid in the brief passage, yet the depth of spiritual intimacy is clear. I find myself wanting to know more, to flesh out the story, and to learn the particulars of Jesus' teaching and her learning at his feet. If nothing else, it is an invitation, particularly to women, to claim the posture of receptivity and learning and to open themselves to the work of discernment.

An even richer paradigm of spiritual direction as teaching is found in the encounter of Jesus with the Samaritan woman at the well. In many ways she is the opposite of Simon the Pharisee: as a woman and a Samaritan, she is relegated to society's margins, a throwaway person. Yet Jesus initiates a conversation with her, beginning with a practical, down-to-earth request for a drink of water and then moves rapidly from the physical to the spiritual:

> Jesus said to her, "Everyone who drinks of this water will be thirsty again, but those who drink of the water that I

> will give them will never be thirsty. The water that I will give will become in them a spring of water gushing up to eternal life." The woman said to him, "Sir, give me this water, so that I may never be thirsty or have to keep coming here to draw water" (Jn. 4:13-15).

Once again, the object of the teaching is self-knowledge: Jesus helps the woman to look into herself deeply and discover her thirst for God.

He surprises her with his knowledge of her sexual life, an area that is personal, private, and potentially shameful. Yet she experiences his candor as liberating, for she leaves her water jar and goes to tell the whole city of her meeting with this prophet who has identified himself to her as the Messiah. John tells us, "Many Samaritans from that city believed in him because of the woman's testimony, 'He told me everything I have ever done'" (v. 39). She does not feel found out or accused, but rather—for the first time—truly known. Now she is free to know herself, see herself, and be herself. In this new freedom, she too becomes a teacher and brings good news to her neighbors, leading them on the first step toward self-knowledge.

There is another important message for spiritual directors in this story: we may find our most receptive directees among the outcasts, those who live at the economic, social, or ecclesiastical edges. These are people who have little to lose and everything to gain. Perhaps they are outcast by birth, chance, or choice. But when Jesus asks the Samaritan woman to give him a drink, he is telling us that there are no outcasts, that the label itself is artificial and unreal.

Like Simon the Pharisee, the Samaritan woman lives on among us. Sometimes she is well dressed and seems to belong, but reveals her status when she lets us glimpse her carefully concealed despair, depression, or addiction. Sometimes we have pushed her to the edges because of ethnicity, sexual orientation, or poverty. If we work at it, we can walk through our days and never see her.

*Chapter Two*
## GOOD TEACHERS

Not long ago I met the Samaritan woman on the uptown C train. It had been a long day, filled with intense conversations and other people's pain. I didn't want to talk to anybody, and I certainly didn't want to listen to anybody. I expected to practice the cure of souls from 8:00 to 5:00, but now I was off duty, and looking forward to the anonymity of the subway, to immersing myself in my paperback.

Then a shabby, disheveled, not very clean woman sat down beside me. I thought, "How can I escape? She's already eyeing my clerical collar; she's spotted me for a soft touch." Sure enough: "How are you, sister?" Then the words rushed out. In a matter of minutes, I seem to have heard the story of her life, her struggle with addiction, her hopes for a new beginning in a rehabilitation center. I knew that I wasn't off duty, after all, so I said what I thought were the right things and felt *very* holy to be so kind. When she got ready to leave, I knew she was going to ask for money and assure me that it was for nourishing food, not drugs. I went through my inner argument: should I, shouldn't I come up with a quarter, maybe two quarters? Then, as she stood up, she leaned close to me and pressed a subway token into my hand. "God bless you, sister." And she was gone.

I had failed to recognize her. My day and my energies had been spent with people who take showers and keep appointments. It had been a good day—at the least, I had probably done no harm. But in retrospect I know that the woman on the subway was thirsty, not for drugs or alcohol, but for a sip of the water that would become in her a spring welling up to eternal life. I had responded with amiable platitudes, but inspite of that she was able to discern Christ in our midst. There was life in her gift to me, and I felt that she "knew everything I ever did" and that it was all right.

*Desert Teachers*
In their extreme asceticism and apparent denial of the goodness of creation, the fathers and mothers of the fourth-century desert seem unlikely mentors for spiritual directors

in our day. Bizarre and often cantankerous, they would be out of place in the well-groomed respectability of our churches. (Abba Pambo said, "The monk should wear a garment of such a kind that he could throw it out of his cell and no one would steal it from him for three days."[2]) Yet as spiritual directors, they were educators in the truest sense of the word, drawing forth insights and understanding from their followers. True learning came from looking inward, facing oneself (and God) in solitude: "Go, sit in your cell, and your cell will teach you everything."[3]

These desert solitaries taught by the example of their own lives as well as by their cryptic counsel. Abba Isaac tells of his search as a young man for a spiritual master. Twice he attached himself to more experienced abbas, ready to live in their households and to serve them. But they did not tell him what to do; rather, *they* served *him*. Isaac turned to other abbas for counsel:

> They came and said to him, "Abba, the brother has come to your holiness in order to help you. Why do you never tell him anything?" The old man said to them, "Am I a cenobite, that I should give him orders? As far as I am concerned, I do not tell him anything, but if he wishes he can do what he sees me doing." From that moment on I [Isaac] took the initiative and did what the old man was about to do. As for him, what he did, he did in silence; so he taught me to work in silence.[4]

They were willing to be silent, indeed, were comfortable in the creative tension of silence. Like Theodore of Pherme, they could resist being made into gurus and were quite happy to be themselves:

> "I meet people as they find me." Then he said to his disciple, "If someone comes to see me, do not say anything out of human respect, but if I am eating, say to him, 'He is eating'; and if I am sleeping, say to him, 'He is sleeping.'"[5]

Most of the spiritual directors of the desert were men, but one of the few women, Amma Theodora, writes about

*Chapter Two*
GOOD TEACHERS

teachers in words directly applicable to twentieth-century spiritual directors:

> A teacher ought to be a stranger to the desire for domination, vain-glory, and pride; one should not be able to fool him by flattery, nor blind him by gifts, nor conquer him by the stomach, nor dominate him by anger; but he should be patient, gentle, and humble as far as possible; he must be tested and without partisanship, full of concern, and a lover of souls.[6]

There is nothing bizarre or cantankerous about Theodora! She knew nothing of the vocabulary of projection, transference, or countertransference, but saw that the director-teacher could get caught in self-deception and lose her loving detachment in a relationship of spiritual intimacy. As directors, our warning bells should also go off when directees bring us adulation rather than respect and try to elevate us to sanctity. Directees rarely attempt to blind me by gifts, or "conquer me by the stomach"—but I resist invitations that are purely social and can trivialize the relationship.

When Theodora warns against anger, she no doubt was thinking of her own, since the abbas and the ammas of the desert struggled constantly against this passion. (Abba Agathon said, "A man who is angry, even if he were to raise the dead, is not acceptable to God."[7]) As a spiritual director, I am in greater danger from other people's anger and my own reaction to it. Most of us want to be liked and are consequently reluctant to offend. Since most people have trouble expressing anger, especially in anything to do with God, we are often faced by testing behavior or denial in our directees when they come to us full of rage. How long do we let it go on? How do we respond, combining love and truth? How can we use the directee's anger?

With Michelle, desperately lonely and still unhealed from a childhood with an abusive mother, the situation is complicated. I know she sees me as a "good" mother, but fears I might turn on her. We have worked together long enough for her to want to test the relationship, and about a year ago, she pushed me further and further toward confrontation. Michelle was consumed by rage and jealousy, which she dared not name and attempted to mask by a pious sweetness. She resisted relationships and experiences that would force her, like Simon the Pharisee, to stop looking at others in harsh judgment and instead see herself clearly. The others—her classmates, fellow parishioners, members of her prayer group—she implied, were nice people but not on her level. If I did not name her spiritual grandiosity (masking an abysmal absence of self-worth), I was guilt of complicity. So I spoke some hard truths, then said: "You're probably really angry at me, and that's all right. It won't hurt me, and I won't get angry at you." With rage in her eyes but in a soft, sweet voice, she assured me that she could never be angry with me. Then she disappeared for six months.

According to Amma Theodora, the director should also be without partisanship. We all want to be favorite children: God's favorites, our parents' favorites, our director's favorite—even when the relationship is one of mutuality and not quasi-parental. (I recall with shame my own sense of betrayal years ago when I learned by chance that I shared my director with a woman whom I considered well-intentioned, but not very bright. "What can she see in *her*?" was my initial reaction.) In the small world of spiritual direction, we often know our directees in other contexts, and our directees are likely to know, possibly dislike, and even feel contempt for each other. Strict observance of confidentiality can help us toward impartiality. If we cannot be open to the directee and even find ourselves taking sides, it is past time to refer her to someone else, taking full responsibility for the deterioration of the relationship.

*Discerning the Questions*

There are many questions in spiritual direction—asked, implied, answered, and unanswered—but as the story gets told and the extraneous stripped away, it is clear that *one* question lies at its heart: "Good Teacher, what must I do to

*Chapter Two*
GOOD TEACHERS

inherit eternal life?" (Mk. 10:17) It is rarely phrased so baldly, and the person seeking spiritual direction may not be aware that it is the central question. The director knows, of course, that the yearning for God and a relationship with God—eternal life—underlies everything in the work of direction and knits the disparate parts together. For the directee, the question may emerge in sharper focus as trust develops and the work continues, but the question has been there all along.

The Gospel of Mark's account of the rich young man is a paradigm for spiritual direction, especially for spiritual direction as teaching. His words of address—"Good Teacher"—acknowledge the hierarchical relationship: he looks to the teacher for an answer he cannot find within himself. There is also an affectionate connection; it is implied that the good teacher will have the interest of the questioner at heart. It seems simplistic to note that one can be a teacher only in relationship, that the whole purpose of teaching is to enable another to make his own discoveries. So the hierarchy is a gentle and perhaps transitory one, and the teacher's apparent power is just that—apparent. As in Mark's story, the questioner must be free to deal with and even learn to love the question.

Mark tells us that "Jesus, looking at him, loved him" (Mk. 10:21). The teacher-pupil relationship is based on love—or should be. We tend to be miserly with our love and to assume its propriety only in close personal relationships. Most damaging of all, we confuse love with warm, mushy, entangling feelings. Such is not the detached, clear-eyed love of the teacher.

I find myself wondering whether the man knew that Jesus loved him. At that moment, probably not! One of the hard tasks of spiritual direction is to learn to speak the truth in love. We may spare the very fragile, those who have already more reality than they can bear and are not yet ready to hear the truth. It is sometimes hard to sit with an insight, yet we may say nothing, or we may measure out manageable bits of truth. But with the strong and spiritually mature, we need not be so cautious.

I learned this in a conversation with Karen, who had come to talk about her growing sense of vocation to the ordained ministry. I knew enough about her family situation and her husband's implacable hostility toward the church to know that her marriage could not withstand the strain, if she decided to pursue her vocation. What I didn't know was Karen's great inner toughness, almost ruthlessness. So I said mildly, rather like "Dear Abby" trying to help make her life run smoothly, "A person really needs family support, especially a spouse's support, before she starts off on this road." Karen's eyes flashed: "I'm talking about a call from *God*!"

I knew then that this was a woman who didn't want minimum doses of sugar-coated truth, so I said, "Excuse me for not saying directly what I meant. You know that your marriage probably won't survive if you pursue the call to ordination, don't you?"

Karen whispered, "I know."

Had the unnamed seeker in Mark's gospel come to me, I might have been tempted to comfort him: "You're really doing fine. Most people wouldn't be able to keep all those commandments! So just keep on doing what you're doing, and don't worry about eternal life." But Jesus knew that this man was ready to hear the truth, and so he gave *the* answer to *the* question. "When he heard this, he was shocked and went away grieving, for he had many possessions" (Mk. 10:22).

Here again, Jesus is the teacher of discernment. He says, "Look at your life. Look at your treasure. See yourself!" What were the young man's many possessions? What are the possessions that weigh down our directees, intruding themselves between the seeker and God? Most obviously, the man was materially wealthy; no doubt in first-century Palestine, as in twentieth-century North America, money management could demand total commitment. Wealth is an attractive idol, easier to get hold of than God and promising comfort and

*Chapter Two*
GOOD TEACHERS

security. But there are other possessions that can cause the seeker to go away grieving. It is hard to let go of carefully maintained identities, especially clerical and "spiritual" ones. (Perhaps this explains why so many clergy are unreliable as directees.) It is hard to let go of a lifetime of accumulated addictions, not merely addictions to harmful chemicals, but also to frantic busyness, mind- and spirit-numbing leisure time activities, and unhealthy relationships. And it is especially hard to let go of the freedom of spiritual irresponsibility, even though drifting aimlessly and ignoring the magnetic pull of God's love brings its own special pain.

The story of the rich man makes clear that spiritual direction is not to be undertaken lightly. Those who see it as yet another avenue toward self-improvement and self-discovery may be surprised at the demands made upon them if they persevere and "follow all the commandments." They may expect a pat on the head; instead, the demands increase as commitment increases. As the work deepens in its intensity, it is important for the spiritual director-teacher to remember what is being taught: to look at oneself without flinching and then to act and be accordingly.

Sometimes the cost is too much, and the directee chooses to leave the relationship. Often the reasons for termination are not articulated, or those given are beside the point. Once a colleague told me the poignant story of a woman who told him the real reason she wouldn't be back. She was well-to-do, leisured, educated—a good woman who observed all the commandments. As my colleague met with her regularly for spiritual direction, he was delighted to watch her grow and find a voice. She was being transformed before his eyes, and he sensed that she stood on a threshold. He didn't know what the next step might be; it might involve a radical change in her way of life, or outwardly she might seem the same, but her whole life would radiate from a deep inner commitment. And then she said, "I won't be back. This is costing too much. I'm going to have to change, and I don't want to change. I like my life the way it is." I don't know about the woman, but my friend came away grieving.

Jesus was able to let the man go. This is a hard lesson for spiritual directors, maybe because we fear "failure." In other words, we have a prideful stake in being right, being effective directors, pointing out the best route. It is hard to let people go and hard to entrust them to God's care—which might mean that our time together will bear fruit decades into the future, but they will wander in a far country and eat husks until then.

*Good Teachers*

We have all had sufficient experience of bad or mediocre teachers to know that, in our human finitude, we must strive to be as-good-as-possible teachers. The responsibility of spiritual direction is a heavy one, and the possibility for mischief is great. What are the marks of a good teacher?

First, *a good teacher encourages play.* Our culture has made leisure an industry, but knows very little about play. Often what we call "play" is competitive or compulsive, because the aesthetic dimension of true play, its holy uselessness, goes against our grain. Yet as the German poet-philosopher Schiller wisely says, the human being is completely human only at play.

I am constantly struck by the proximity of "play" and "pray"; this is brought home to me in serendipitous messages from my word processor, when my fingers take on a life of their own and I find myself writing, "It will be necessary to play about this." The linking of play and prayer—and implicitly, the linking of play with the work of contemplative living—is apparent in the fourteenth-century mystical work, *The Cloud of Unknowing.* The author notes that it is not always possible to be at one's spiritual best:

> Sickness, afflictions of body and mind, and countless other necessities of nature will often leave you indisposed and keep you from prayer's heights. Yet, at the same time, I

*Chapter Two*
GOOD TEACHERS

>    counsel you to remain at it always either in earnest or, as it were, *playfully.* [Emphasis added.][8]

These are reassuring words for director-teachers trying to help their directees through periods of aridity, poor health, personal difficulties, and distraction. Directees may make heavy going of it and add a load of self-blame to the burden they are already carrying. Others tend to slack off when it is not possible to maintain the level of spiritual intensity they have set for themselves, with the result that they turn away from spiritual direction at the time when it could be of the greatest support. The director can help them remain at it "as it were, playfully." A light touch is called for:

>    For the love of God, then, be careful and do not imprudently strain yourself at this work. Rely more on joyful enthusiasm than on sheer brute force....Do not impatiently snatch at grace like a greedy greyhound suffering from starvation.[9]

The anonymous author of the *Ancrene Riwle* presents a delightful picture of prayer as play, a game of hide and seek with a playful parent God, who "is playing with us as a mother with her darling child." No sooner does the child look around and call for her than she runs back, her arms outstretched, and embraces him.

>    In the same way, Our Lord sometimes leaves us alone for a while and withdraws His grace, his comfort and consolation, so that we find no pleasure in doing things well, and our heart's savour is gone. And yet, at that very moment our Lord is not loving us any the less, but is doing this out of his great love for us.[10]

Play is at once intense (just watch a four-year-old with Matchbox cars and a few blocks!) and liberating. We are freed from our compulsion for right answers, freed from the need to acquire and achieve, freed from anxiety by the transitory nature of play. With imagination as the generous supplier of raw materials, we can be rich beyond belief. Everything matters tremendously—and not at all. Furthermore, since it is

# HOLY LISTENING
*The Art of Spiritual Direction*

hard to be heavily defended when engaged in true play, it is also an excellent way of shedding our masks and letting ourselves be known, of *unselfing*, in the classical language of spirituality. Play stretches us and helps push out the boundaries; in spiritual direction, it can provide gentle help in discarding icons that have turned into homemade idols. For that matter, it can also provide the exhilarating energy with which—in our younger days—we knocked down block structures and sand castles when they had served their purpose.

So play has a real place in the serious work of spiritual direction, and I try to find ways to introduce it. This calls for gentle perseverance; although some directees don't mind—or even welcome—"penitential assignments," they are frightened at the prospect of play. So when I suggested that Alice make a list of at least three ways in which God might delight in her, she declared she couldn't think of one single thing. Even contemplating the exercise seemed presumptuous to her until I reminded her of the verse tucked into the middle of Psalm 18: "He brought me out into a broad place; he delivered me, because he delighted in me" (v. 19). I encouraged her to play with the idea, to pay attention to the small, seemingly trivial things that came into her mind. At our next meeting, she announced with a smile that God might delight in her tennis game, her pleasant voice, and the fact that she had managed to complete college while working part-time.

Grace proved more difficult. She lives—rather grimly—for her family and was angrily resistant when I suggested that she play with a plan of what she would do if she had only herself to consider. "Are you telling me to imagine that my family is dead?" she asked. Her resistance tells me a great deal about her image of God—and her true feelings about her family. I haven't been brave enough to suggest Psalm 18 to her yet.

Sometimes it helps if I enter into the play, carefully, so that the directee does not feel compelled to imitate me but rather

*Chapter Two*
GOOD TEACHERS

is free to find his own voice and images. This has proved effective in groups when the members get stuck in safe and pious platitudes. Once I was working with a group of women and suggested that we play with the idea of God's names and images for us. We were having trouble getting past "beloved child" and "faithful servant" when I said, "You know, I think God sees me as a little gray donkey, hardworking, pretty reliable, but awfully thick-headed." After the laughter died down, we found that the group was flooded with images—powerful, comic, poignant. We were letting ourselves be known.

Directees who resist play in spiritual direction often combine a poor self-image with a tendency to "spiritualize" everything. In other words, they want to avoid the grittiness of everyday life and so come to see me expecting pious conversation divorced from all reality. With wicked humor the author of *The Cloud* says of such displays of piety, "Sometimes their eyes look like the eyes of wounded sheep near death" and goes on to counsel avoidance of the extreme and the eccentric: "Far better a modest countenance, a calm, composed bearing, and a merry candor."[11]

Here the spiritual director can help to sanctify the ordinary and restore naturalness. "A merry candor" is better taught by example than by precept, and the director can begin by demythologizing himself. If he is a man who is ordained, he might substitute mufti for clerical garb when meeting with the excessively spiritual. This is also a good time for some judicious self-revelation, connecting the life of prayer with the minutiae of the here and now. Sometimes it helps for the directee to know that I go to the grocery store or visit my dentist. I still remember my daughter's surprise at meeting her nursery school teacher in the supermarket—it had not occurred to her that Miss Pat shopped, cooked, and ate like ordinary mortals. So an occasional bit of down-to-earth chat as we say goodbye can go a long way toward helping the directee remember that I, like Miss Pat, am an ordinary mortal.

# HOLY LISTENING
*The Art of Spiritual Direction*

*A good teacher knows the pupil's limits.* This calls for great sensitivity to timing, knowing when to speak and when to keep silent. It is tempting to turn teaching into instruction, but we are not there to tell people things, to help them to analyze themselves; instead, we are there to *educate*, literally, to help them bring forth what is already there. The work of discernment is different with each one: the newly baptized person, still in the euphoria of a conversion experience, merits quite different treatment from the third-year seminarian who possesses a sophisticated theological vocabulary and a certain cynicism about the institutional church. The former needs the gentle support of someone willing to share in his joy and to encourage him not to push on too quickly, while the seminarian may need to be challenged not to hide behind intellectual abstractions. She might well welcome a certain toughness of approach that would be out of place with a newcomer.

People coming to spiritual direction for the first time often say, "I need somebody who won't let me get away with anything, somebody tough. I don't want somebody who's just going to be nice to me." When I first began this work, I trembled inwardly and thought, "This is a strong person who can see right through me and knows that I'm a pussy cat if not an outright wimp. Who do I know who's *really* tough?" Now that I have heard variations of the same request dozens, even hundreds of times, however, I am better able to see the wounded, tentative seeker behind the bravado and to know that this is a person who feels unworthy of God's love. Not long ago I met with Jean, an attractive woman who seemed to have it all: professional success, a secure marriage, handsome children. Her manner was friendly but brisk, her language precise. She hoped that I would be able to refer her to a director who would challenge and confront her, not let her get away with anything. (Those words again!) I decided to take the risk, so after a moment I asked, "Why are you afraid of gentleness, Jean?" Tears came into her eyes, and she shook her head.

*Chapter Two*
GOOD TEACHERS

Still, the director needs to combine gentleness with candor and expect commitment and hard work from the directee. A good teacher demands accountability, which is why we usually learn better with a teacher than we do on our own, no matter what the subject matter. But this accountability is mutual, with no place in it for fear or coercion. I am accountable to the directee, to whom I owe my attention, discretion, and prayers, while she is accountable through taking the relationship seriously, honoring the director's gift of time and attention, and bringing her best and truest self to the work.

<u>A good teacher is always hopeful</u>. I am convinced that much of the grimness of contemporary secular education exists because it is a loveless enterprise from which no fruit is really expected. The teacher/director, on the other hand, is filled with hope for the directee. Seeing the potential for growth and transformation in even the least likely, he is willing to wait for fruition. In dark times, his quiet hope can sustain the directee. This is the hopefulness of Dame Julian who, without shrinking from pain and evil, knew that ultimately all would be well. God

> did not say: You will not be troubled, you will not be belaboured, you will not be disquieted; but he said: You will not be overcome. God wants us to pay attention to these words, and always to be strong in faithful trust, in well-being and in woe, for he loves and delights in us, and so he wishes us to love him and delight in him and trust greatly in him, and all will be well.[12]

In one of his homilies, Gregory the Great depicts Jesus as a teacher who encourages and sustains hope. He speaks movingly of John's account of Mary Magdalene's perseverance at the empty tomb:

> Why did she stoop down again, why did she want to look again? It is never enough for a lover to have looked once, because love's intensity does not allow a lover to give up the search. Mary sought a first time and found nothing; she persevered in seeking, and so it happened that she found Jesus.[13]

HOLY LISTENING
*The Art of Spiritual Direction*

How often directees look into the empty tomb, even when they "know" it is empty. This calls for patience on the part of the director and awareness that the directee is in the right place for now, even though it is painful to linger in a place that seems dead and fruitless. Our tendency is to want to get on with it, whatever "it" might be. We both see the tomb is empty, so come on, let's go! But here the pupil is wise, knowing what she must do. She lingers, stoops to look in once again, and "so it happened that she found Jesus."

Mary of Magdalene reminds me of my friend Ellen—I dare not call her a directee, for she is my teacher as much as I am hers. In her nineties and knowing that death is near, like Mary she perseveres in looking into the empty tomb. She does not fear death, but she yearns for a sense of the presence of God after a lifetime of seeking. For a time, with the false wisdom of relative youth and with great confidence in my supposed gift of discernment, I thought she was stuck and needed rescuing from her fruitless search. How could she doubt God's love for her? What more could she want? But I have learned to honor her faithfulness in looking into the empty tomb and to honor my position standing beside (and a little behind) her. She is looking for God, not finding God, but willing to go on waiting and looking.

Gregory reminds us of the importance of Jesus' identity as teacher:

> Because Mary was called by name, she acknowledged her Creator, and called him at once *Rabboni, which means teacher.* He was at once the one she was outwardly seeking, and the one who was inwardly teaching her to seek him.[14]

In his appearance to Mary at the empty tomb, Jesus reminds us powerfully of the object of his teaching and indeed of the teaching of all spiritual directors: he was "inwardly teaching Mary to seek him." Similarly, our true work is neither to impart information nor to support a change in the directee's lifestyle, however desirable these aims might be. Our work is to follow Christ's example and inwardly teach those who come to us to seek him. The prayer of Mary at the empty

*Chapter Two*
GOOD TEACHERS

tomb, and indeed of all engaged in the ministry of spiritual direction, might well be Julian's:

> God, of your goodness, give me yourself, for you are enough for me, and I can ask nothing less which can pay you full worship. And if I ask anything less, always I am in want, but only in you do I have everything.[15]

*A good teacher asks questions*, but they must be the right questions—ones that open doors, invite the directee to stretch and grow. Obviously, one never asks questions out of curiosity, nor to fill a silence that threatens to become uncomfortable, but at times clarification is needed. Then a gentle question can be helpful to director and directee alike: "Could you say a little more about that? Can you give me an example of what you mean by...?" I am learning to notice statements that cry out for a clarifying question, especially when the directee encounters painful material or stands on the threshold of a new stage of awareness. Hints are dropped, bits of information are offered, and the narrative seems disjointed, almost as if the directee were saying: "I left a piece out there. What I am saying doesn't make sense. Why don't you ask me about it?" The clarifying question is by no means probing or pouncing but a simple "Help me understand what you are saying. Do you mean... ?" In the ministry of spiritual direction, there are no right answers, only clearer visions and ever deeper questions.

In awareness of the mystery at the heart of spiritual direction, the good teacher also encourages directees to discover and embrace their own questions. The poet Rilke's *Letters to a Young Poet*, while ostensibly about the creative process, is equally valuable as a spiritual classic. It is a deceptively simply book about discernment and self-knowledge. In the fourth letter, Rilke urges his reader

> to be patient toward all that is unsolved in your heart and to try to love the questions themselves like locked rooms and like books that are written in a very foreign tongue. Do not seek the answers, which cannot be given you because

you would not be able to live them. And the point is, to live everything. Live the questions now.[16]

To love the questions is to engage them ever more deeply, to let go, and to risk. It is to struggle with the translation of "books written in a very foreign tongue"—and to love the struggle. To live the questions is to be willing to persevere in peering into the empty tomb. Directees who come to us wanting a quick fix of spiritual certainty will be sorely disappointed.

*A good teacher is willing and able to evaluate progress.* Even as there are no right answers in spiritual direction, there are no report cards with letter grades. Yet our directees come to us—at least in part—for orientation, to try to understand where they are spiritually, how they got there, and what the next step might be. Like New York's former mayor, we all want to ask, "How'm I doing?" But given our natural bent for self-deception, we need the help of another in making the assessment.

When should you give feedback in spiritual direction? In theory, I think regular times of mutual assessment are helpful, perhaps quarterly, once the relationship is well established. In practice, however, I work pragmatically and often intuitively. Sometimes the directee will ask, "What do you see? Tell me what you think." There is a graced quality to the timing of these requests; almost always we have worked together long enough and intensively enough for me to be able to respond constructively.

Sometimes I offer feedback when the directee seems stuck, not persevering at looking into the empty tomb, but just plain stuck. She may have reached a plateau where faithfulness doesn't seem to be enough. Discouraged, she feels as if she is slipping backward. Then it helps for the director to comment, as specifically as possible, on the growth and change that he has observed. This assessment should be an honest and realistic one, for the aim is not to make the directee feel good but to provide a helpful evaluation.

*Chapter Two*
## GOOD TEACHERS

Occasionally the evaluation is a painful one. After working for some months with Helena, I observed a pattern of envy in her relationship with women clergy. Helena aspired to ordination herself, but had been rejected for the process by her diocese. When we first met, she was enthusiastic about the female curate in her parish, but then her adulation turned to harsh criticism. Helena moved to another parish, where the process repeated itself. When she told me that she was think of changing parishes again, and commented (as if introducing a new topic) that the young woman assistant was a poor preacher and *very* hard to talk to, I knew it was time to point out what I was seeing. Helena hasn't changed parishes again; she is somewhat more realistic about the capabilities and deficiencies of the women clergy, and considerably more aware of the depths of her own disappointment and its potential for poisoning her relationship with others.

Feedback is especially welcome to those who have had a profound religious experience and are reluctant to name it. I never cease to be surprised at our circumspection in speaking of God, particularly a sense of God's immanence, even in spiritual direction. Jeff had come to me seeking a referral for a director. He was down-to-earth, matter-of-fact, and definitely not unbalanced. But as he talked, it was clear to me that he was gifted with mystical experiences and was afraid to talk about them, probably for fear that he would be seen as eccentric, if not downright demented. Finally, I said, "It sounds as if you are very blessed. Lots of people would envy your experience of God's nearness." He looked surprised, then laughed with relief when I said, "I guess it's safe to say the dreaded M-word—mystical." He still holds his secret very close, an indication to me that his mystical tendencies are healthy and genuine. The "M-word" has become a code expression between us.

<u>A good teacher is vulnerable</u>. She bears her own partially healed wounds and scars and counts them among her gifts. Annie Sullivan, Helen Keller's teacher, provides a good model. When she began to work with Helen, Annie herself

# HOLY LISTENING
*The Art of Spiritual Direction*

was young and seriously impaired, but her handicap made her available to the isolated child and enabled her to make demands the "whole" and "healthy" members of the Keller family were unable to make. Helen's name for this woman, who enabled her to know and be known, was "Teacher."

Many of us are Annie Sullivans when we begin the work of spiritual direction, spiritually if not chronologically young, and afflicted with imperfect vision. It is tempting to deny our gifts for this ministry and to wait, in the expectation that someday we will be ready—strong, unblemished, and wise. How do you know when you are ready to be a spiritual director? The best indication is that people begin to seek you out to talk about their deepest concerns and are willing to lay aside their masks when they are with you. This can be a heady experience, and one should be wary if it is *too* enjoyable. It cannot be said too often that the director needs to be humble, i.e., know her own small place in the great order of things. Given true humility and the safeguard of having her own director, the reluctant novice can increase and deepen her skills in the ministry.

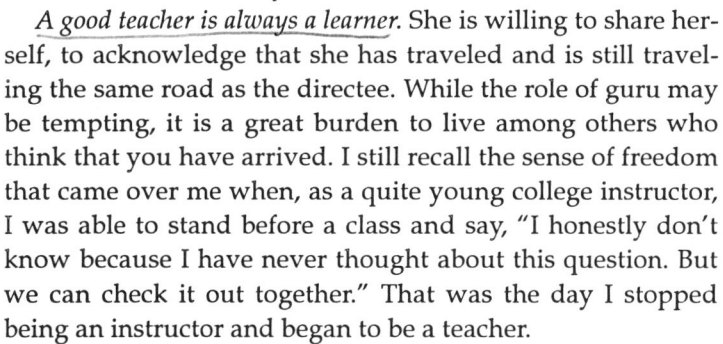

*A good teacher is always a learner.* She is willing to share herself, to acknowledge that she has traveled and is still traveling the same road as the directee. While the role of guru may be tempting, it is a great burden to live among others who think that you have arrived. I still recall the sense of freedom that came over me when, as a quite young college instructor, I was able to stand before a class and say, "I honestly don't know because I have never thought about this question. But we can check it out together." That was the day I stopped being an instructor and began to be a teacher.

In the seminar room and in spiritual direction, danger arises when the teacher stops learning. The mutuality of the teacher-learner relationship is lost, as one has and gives, the other is empty and receives. Instead, as Aelred points out, there should be a circularity in the exchange: "Speak freely, therefore, and entrust to your friend all your cares and thoughts, that you may both learn and teach, give and

*Chapter Two*
GOOD TEACHERS

receive, pour out and drink in."[17] The teacher who lets herself be taught will always be aware of what the other is experiencing and know what it is like to be in the learner's position. It was an illuminating experience for me when, after years in the classroom, I resumed piano lessons. But this was a pale foreshadowing of what it was like, at age fifty, to move from the teacher's position of authority behind the desk and join my fellow juniors in seminary!

*A good teacher (like a good parent) is educating for maturity.* Parents have done their work well when they are no longer needed. In spiritual direction, a relationship that is initially hierarchical may turn into a rich spiritual friendship. This is not a sign that something has gone wrong, but it is important to acknowledge and celebrate the changed relationship. The friendship can continue, but the directee will eventually need to find a new director. The give-and-take between friends cannot substitute for the careful attentiveness of a lovingly distanced director.

*The Teacher of Prayer*

The purpose of spiritual direction resembles a statement Thomas Merton once made about the purpose of education—to help us define ourselves authentically and spontaneously in relation to our world.[18] The purpose of spiritual direction is similar—to help people discover how to define themselves in relation not only to the world, but also to God. That is a huge and seemingly amorphous undertaking, the work of a lifetime. But within this framework, the director is called upon to help in specific ways, to teach in an almost traditional manner.

When I ask people why they wish to enter spiritual direction, most often their answer has something to do with prayer. "I need help in prayer. I want to deepen my prayer life. I want to learn to pray better." They feel they do not pray enough and want either to be scolded or excused for their deficiencies. More important still is their sense that they are somehow not praying correctly, with the implication that there is a right way or a secret recipe, something that can be taught them cognitively.

While that consummate teacher of prayer, the author of *The Cloud* and *The Book of Privy Counseling*, is making a strong case for what we now know as "centering prayer," he seems also to be acknowledging that there are different temperaments and needs, and hence no single right way to pray:

> Do not pray with words unless you are really drawn to this; or if you do pray with words, pay no attention to whether they are many or few. Do not weigh them in their meaning. Do not be concerned about what kind of prayers you use, for it is unimportant whether or not they are official liturgical prayers, psalms, hymns, or anthems; whether they are for particular or general intentions; or whether you formulate them interiorly, by thoughts, or express them aloud, in words.[19]

Essential only is that there be "a naked intent stretching out toward God." These are good precepts to be borne in mind by the spiritual director who is a teacher of prayer. I have to avoid trying to make directees over in my own image. What works for me right now may not be right for someone else. We are often tempted, especially when our own prayer is going well, to prescribe our method to everyone.

Books on prayer can be helpful, but should be prescribed cautiously because it is easy to substitute reading *about* prayer for the prayer itself. Furthermore, most directees will obediently read and try to adopt whatever we suggest even if it is not suitable. Worse still, they may *not* follow the suggestion and then feel guilty at their own "disobedience," thus increasing feelings of inadequacy and failure rather than mitigating them.

Teaching about prayer always involves a task of discernment. Should the directee be encouraged to persevere with a method of prayer even though it seems stale and difficult, or is it time for a radically new approach? Sometimes seeming fruitlessness is a sign that a breakthrough is about to take place, while at other times it means that the directee is per-

*Chapter Two*
GOOD TEACHERS

sisting in outgrown ways and needs to be encouraged to stretch, grow, and take risks.

Sometimes less is more. Spiritual gluttony is a danger, especially if the person comes to spiritual direction from a recent conversion experience or is addicted to what my English friend Janet calls "little books." Filling one's shelves with books about prayer is a poor substitute for prayer itself, and immersing oneself in other people's recipes for the spiritual life is an effective delaying tactic. Then the prescription of faithfulness and simplicity is in order. A recent seminary graduate assures me that I once told her to stay out of chapel for a while after she confided in me that her over-conscientious attendance at community services was causing her own rich life of contemplative prayer to dry up.

I prefer to give suggestions rather than specific assignments. "You might try this" or "This has been helpful to me" is usually enough to open the way for new approaches. As noted above, the proximity of *pray* and *play* is too striking to be overlooked. The directee can be encouraged to explore his personal images for God. This is especially liberating for those who find the accepted liturgical language overwhelmingly patriarchal. It may take a while to convince them that, in solitary prayer, they are free to find their own images and terms of address for God and that they are indeed in excellent company. (One need think only of Julian's "Jesus our mother" and Teresa of Avila's "Majesty.")

For directees who claim they never have to time to pray, we can encourage them to find new places and occasions. Two of my favorite holy places are the subway and the kitchen, although both could be seen as spiritually empty, waste spaces. The subway, where we cannot escape the sight of the wounded Body of Christ, is a fruitful place for prayers of intercession, while repetitive tasks in the kitchen can be sanctified by the Jesus Prayer. Directees can be encouraged to pray while walking or before opening a book in the library or while performing manual labor. One colleague tells me that he combines centering prayer with his daily half-hour of running.

There are so many avenues—praying imaginatively in the Ignatian way or following the author of *The Cloud* in imageless prayer; praying with the aid of icons, crucifixes, candles, and rosaries; praying standing, sitting, kneeling, and prostrate; praying through keeping a journal; praying the Jesus Prayer of the Heart; letting Scripture speak to us through the method of *lectio divina*. It is a rich feast, and it is important for the director to be sparing with suggestions. Too much at once is an excessively lavish buffet at which spiritual indigestion and spiritual gluttony are both real dangers.

People also come to spiritual direction seeking aid in formulating a rule of life. While some, particularly those attracted to monasticism, articulate this clearly in traditional religious terms, the desire for help in shaping and structuring the daily routine is implicit in almost every case. Most rules are quasi-monastic, dealing chiefly with the allotment and nature of prayer time; liturgical observance, such as regular attendance at the Eucharist and perhaps the Sacrament of Reconciliation; and some form of accountability, such as a formal association with a religious order, ongoing meetings with a Cursillo group, or periodic meetings with a spiritual director. In other words, what is the pattern of the specifically "religious" parts of one's life?

Henry, for example, arrives in my office with a concise, tidy list: he will be present at the Eucharist on Sunday, spend twenty minutes a day in centering prayer, make an annual three-day retreat at a nearby convent, and make his confession in Advent and Lent. He isn't really asking for my help in forming his rule; he just wants my approval. It's a good enough rule, in a traditional sense, for it provides an intentional basis for a life lived in awareness of God.

But a good rule goes beyond the narrowly devotional. If we are to be whole people, it must be more than a schedule for our visiting hours with God. I can tell by looking at Henry that he doesn't get any exercise, and I remember his

*Chapter Two*
GOOD TEACHERS

discomfort at the absence of ashtrays from my office, yet he has left no place in his rule for care and restoration of his body. I know too, from our conversations, that his marriage has become grim and silent. I'm delighted at his plan to spend three days in the convent, but feel impelled to suggest that he devote a similar long weekend to his wife, away from household cares, in the best resort hotel he can afford.

There is a common tendency to try to take on too much, to try to live a monastic life amidst the stimuli and pressures of the everyday late twentieth-century world. Instead of retreating to a quiet oratory for morning prayer, many people begin their day with an hour on the interstate or in crowded public transportation. Can the rule of life be adapted to turn a commute into a place and time of prayer? How does one manage extended periods of contemplative prayer when there is a new baby in the house, and perhaps a few toddlers underfoot as well? A rule of life for people living in families, where each member is at a different place spiritually, calls for creativity and flexibility. And most of us live with the absence of community support; it is a painful fact that seriously observant Christians are in the minority in our society.

Someone once likened a rule of life to a rose trellis. Its purpose is to support, to set us free from the tyranny of "shoulds" and "oughts," in other words, to set us free for growth. As such, it is an instrument to be used and adapted, rather than a monument carved in stone.

A good rule deals with traditional matters of devotional practice, but goes further to encompass the stewardship of energy, creativity, and time. We are a time-obsessed people in a way unthinkable to the author of *The Cloud*, who cautions:

> Be attentive to time and the way you spend it. Nothing is more precious. This is evident when you recall that in one tiny moment heaven may be gained or lost. God, the master of time, never gives the future. He gives only the present, moment by moment...[20]

Most people in spiritual direction value their time, protest vigorously that they do not have enough of it, and would

HOLY LISTENING
*The Art of Spiritual Direction*

probably deny that they waste it. Yet the commandment to observe the Sabbath is routinely—even proudly—violated by many of us who are meticulous in our observance of the other nine. "Not wasting time" becomes an excuse for neglecting time for true rest and reflection, what the poet Lessing called "the creative pause." Most importantly, we can use busyness and crowded schedules to hide from God. Even as we delude ourselves that we are being good stewards, we fill our days so tightly that we close God out. Our excessive busyness masks the sin of sloth.

As directors, we work with time-conscious men and women who may already feel guilty about not having time to pray. While they may be responsible stewards of their substance, they need a workable rule of life to bring proportion to their stewardship of time and energy. I sometimes ask people to keep a careful record of their activities, hour by hour, for one day—or better still, for a week. This is analogous to the helpful practice of weight loss programs in which dieters record each morsel of food. In both cases, there are surprises. The person who "eats nothing" discovers that she has been eating all day, taking in a highly caloric mouthful here, a highly caloric mouthful there. The person who would like to pray but "has no time" may find that he is able to watch reruns of "The Odd Couple" and never misses "L.A. Law." So when the log of activity is examined, it will reveal soft places, waste, and evasions.

The directee is able to see time as a precious gift, to be used and structured. Then it is time to create a rule that takes into account the relationship to God, others, and one's deepest self. Areas of disproportion and hence potential sinfulness become apparent, so that the rule can serve as a reminder where caution is needed. Self-care is a holy obligation, yet a surprising number of people formulate a rule that stipulates how many minutes a day will be spent in prayer or how many times a week they will be present at the Eucharist, but ignore their dangerous addictions to food, alcohol, or nicotine. Finally, there needs to be provision for sheer fun. It

*Chapter Two*
GOOD TEACHERS

was a joyous insight when I realized that in Middle English "silly" meant "blessed," cognate with the modern German *selig*. So I find myself asking directees, "What have you put in this rule for fun? Where's the blessed silliness in it?"

*Homework?*

I have already noted my reluctance to *assign* spiritual reading. The directee may dutifully plough through the book, looking in vain for its application to her own situation, or she will not attempt it at all. In either case, I have added a burden and increased the risk of dependency in the relationship, whereby it becomes more important to please me than to discover together what is pleasing to God. Further, all too many people already live in their heads and use the cognitive as a way of avoiding the experience of God. There is nothing wrong with suggesting books that will help them be better informed scripturally, theologically, or historically, so long as both of us are clear about what we are doing and do not let the spiritual direction meetings turn into an inquirers' class. Directees who are intellectually hungry can be encouraged to participate more fully in their parish's education program or urged to take a course in the diocesan school of theology. Most seminaries welcome part-time students, and denominational lines can be easily crossed.

While I rarely assign, I frequently suggest: "This book spoke to me; you might find it helpful too. But don't feel you have to stick with it if it doesn't feel right." It is important that the suggestion be offered very lightly and then dropped. Sometimes it bears fruit slowly. A directee recently came to my study, full of enthusiasm about a book I had mentioned over a year ago. She confessed that she had stopped to buy it at the seminary bookstore on her way home, looked at it briefly and, finding it almost incomprehensible, put it on the shelf. A year later she took it down and discovered that it was just what she needed. Her timing was better than mine!

I always encourage people to read the Bible, not beginning with Genesis and ending with the almost inevitable break-

# HOLY LISTENING
*The Art of Spiritual Direction*

down in Leviticus or—for the truly tenacious—in Chronicles. Rather, I invite them to begin with one of the gospels and to read it through as if it were a long-awaited bestseller. This shocks the pious, who heretofore have read Scripture "devotionally," that is, with their minds turned off and their emotions deadened. But it also awakens them to the vitality of the Bible and the connection of their own story with that of the Gospel. Next I suggest psalms, pointing out that while the 23rd offers familiar comfort, Psalm 88 might be more realistic for certain moods.

> You have laid me in the depths of the Pit,
>   In dark places, and in the abyss.
> Your anger weighs upon me heavily,
>   and all your great waves overwhelm me.
> You have put my friends far from me;
>   you have made me to be abhorred by them;
>   I am in prison and cannot get free.

For those who have trouble acknowledging their own anger, the extravagent vengefulness of Psalm 58 is an eye-opener:

> O, God, break their teeth in their mouths;
>   pull the fangs of the young lions, O LORD.
> Let them vanish like water that runs off;
>   Let them wither like the trodden grass.
> Let them be like the snail that melts away,
>   like a stillborn child that never sees the sun.

It is vastly freeing for directees to become aware of the range of human emotion in the psalms, often a liberating surprise for those who are fearful of expressing doubt, despair, or rage.

Other kinds of "homework" can also form a bridge between our meetings. I have already noted the importance of encouraging the directee to explore new ways, times, and places of praying, especially when the present practices have become perfunctory.

Frequently, my assignment is to "lighten up," not to turn prayer into a work but to listen for God and let oneself be

*Chapter Two*
GOOD TEACHERS

surprised. Overly rigid adherence to a spiritual discipline built around formal liturgical observance and highly structured prayer time can work against the sanctification of the ordinary. Christ is effectively imprisoned, to be visited at stated times and otherwise ignored. So I might suggest listening for God during a walk on a dirty city street, in the quiet of the country, or perhaps in a few minutes of cuddling an infant or a child.

In our tendency to spiritualize we neglect our bodies. Particularly in my work with seminarians, I find myself inquiring about nutrition, exercise, and sleep habits, and I border on the authoritarian in discussions of self-care. Directees limited by chronic or debilitating illness need to be reminded that driving themselves to the limit of endurance is destructive, not heroic. Arthur, who suffers from a degenerative disease and whose prognosis is poor, needs help in overcoming his denial. He sees his illness as a divinely sent test (if not an affliction) and is determined to carry on as if it did not exist. It is hard for him to ask for help and even harder to care for himself when his coordination fails and his body cries out for rest. He berates himself for unfaithfulness when an episode of ill health forces him to curtail, even temporarily, his volunteer work in a homeless shelter. It is hard work to lead him to love his own ailing body as much as he loves the guests at the shelter.

A certain bossiness on my part regarding self-care seems to be welcome, as if the directee were saying to himself, "If my spiritual director says I must, then I really must go for a run or play a game of tennis. And it's a matter of holy obedience to get a sitter at least twice a month so that I can spend an evening alone with my wife." There is a certain playful complicity: the directee and I both know that the "assignment" is really a permission, a permission that wouldn't be necessary if he were able to honor and care for himself as a part of creation.

Most frequently my assignments are to "think about" something. I invite the directee to think about her images of

HOLY LISTENING
*The Art of Spiritual Direction*

God, God's possible images for her, the stepping stones or turning points in her life, the lovely or not so lovely skins she may have shed at each point of transformation. I urge people to make a list, or at least notes, because writing fosters focus and specificity. I have to work hard to remember that some people find writing a burden, so that the mere suggestion of a journal constricts the flow of thought and images. I urge them to find their own way here—perhaps writing in a beautifully bound little book with a proper fountain pen, perhaps using a word processor, maybe even a tape recorder.

Finally, I ask directees to be attentive to causes for celebration in their lives. This can be hard work, especially when they feel they are abandoned by God and living at the bottom of a pit. Some gentle humor helps here, as does the memory of Corrie ten Boom. The devout Dutch woman and her sister Betsie were attempting to obey Paul's injunction to the Thessalonians to give thanks for all things, even the circumstances of their imprisonment in the Nazi concentration camp at Ravensbruck:

> "Thank you," Betsie went on serenely, "for the fleas and for—"
> The fleas! That was too much. "Betsie, there's no way even God can make me grateful for a flea."
> "'Give thanks in *all* circumstances,'" she quoted. "It doesn't say, 'in pleasant circumstances.' Fleas are part of this place where God has put us."[21]

Later the sisters discovered why they and the other women had been relatively free of harassment from the camp guards: their barracks room was crawling with fleas, and the guards feared contagion.

It should be clear that our directees aren't expected to live up to Corrie's heroic sanctity, nor should we encourage them to seek and enjoy suffering. But almost everyone is tormented by some version of Corrie's fleas. Indeed, spiritual fleas may be much harder to bear than more spectacular ills. The pesky little critters lose their power, however, if—lightly,

*Chapter Two*
GOOD TEACHERS

ironically, even with chagrin—we and our directees can give thanks for them as "part of the place where God has put us."

*The Slow Work of God*

"Some brothers...went to see Abba Felix and they begged him to say a word to them. But the old man kept silence. After they had asked him for a long time he said to them, 'You wish to hear a word?' They said, 'Yes, abba.' Then the old man said to them, 'There are no more words nowadays.'"[22]

When people come to us for spiritual direction, we usually assume that—like the abba's disciples—they expect a profound, even life-changing, word from us. But spiritual directors, like all good teachers, need to live with the silence, not merely to endure it but to be comfortable with it. If we are to assist people in the work of knowing and being known, to define themselves authentically and spontaneously in relation to God and their world, then we must be willing to wait with them and often to acknowledge that there are no words.

Silence is rarely comfortable. We are accustomed to wanting certainty and clarity. Yet in the silence, we embrace ambiguity and darkness. People who come for spiritual direction often want answers, want even to be told what to do, but if they persevere, they discover that the darkness and silence increase rather than decrease. In seeking answers, they find that their questions proliferate. The great central question remains: Good teacher, what must I do to inherit eternal life?

Yet as they explore it, moving toward its heart, the mystery deepens. Spiritual directors do well to recall Rilke's advice to the young poet: to love and to live the questions. Good teachers love questions because they love the mystery of locked rooms and books that are written in a very foreign tongue, and the need for almost infinite patience and trust "in the slow work of God."

# Endnotes

1 Parker Palmer, *To Know As We Are Known: A Spirituality of Education* (San Francisco: Harper & Row, 1983), p. 31.

2 Ward, *Desert Christian*, p. 197.

3 *Ibid.*, p. 139.

4 *Ibid.*, pp. 99-100.

5 *Ibid.*, p. 78.

6 *Ibid.*, pp. 83-84.

7 *Ibid.*, p. 23.

8 *The Cloud of Unknowing and The Book of Privy Counseling*, ed. William Johnston (Garden City, NY: Image Books, 1973), p. 100.

9 *Ibid.*, pp. 106-107.

10 *The Ancrene Riwle*, trans. M. B. Salu (London: Burns & Oates, 1955), p. 134.

11 *The Cloud of Unknowing*, p. 116.

12 Julian of Norwich, p. 315.

13 Gregory the Great, *Be Friends of God*, ed. John Leinenweber, (Cambridge, MA: Cowley, 1990), pp. 27-28.

14 *Ibid.*, p. 56.

15 Julian of Norwich, p. 184.

16 Rainer Maria Rilke, *Letters to a Young Poet*, trans. M. D. Herter Norton (New York: W. W. Norton, 1954), p. 35.

17 Aelred, *Friendship*, p. 52.

18 Thomas Merton, *Love and Living* (New York: Farrar Straus & Giroux, 1979), p. 3.

19 *The Cloud*, p. 149.

20 *Ibid*, pp. 50-51.

21 Corrie ten Boom, *The Hiding Place*, pp. 198-199.

22 Ward, *Desert Christian*, p. 242.

CHAPTER THREE

# Midwife to the Soul

Tend only to the birth in you and you will find all goodness and all consolation, all delight, all being and all truth. Reject it and you reject goodness and blessing. What comes to you in this birth brings with it pure being and blessing. But what you seek or love outside of this birth will come to nothing, no matter what you will or where you will it.
*Meister Eckhart*

Now there was a Pharisee named Nicodemus, a leader of the Jews. He came to Jesus by night and said to him, "Rabbi, we know that you are a teacher who has come from God; for no one can do these signs you do apart from the presence of God." Jesus answered him, "Very truly, I tell you, no one can see the kingdom of God without being born from above." Nicodemus said to him, "How can anyone be born after having grown old? Can one enter a second time into the mother's womb and be born?"
*John 3:1-4*

# Midwife to the Soul

The king of Egypt said to the Hebrew midwives, one of whom was named Shiphrah and the other Puah, "When you serve as midwives to the Hebrew women, and see them on the birthstool, if it is a boy, kill him; but if it is a girl, she shall live." But the midwives feared God; they did not do as the king of Egypt commanded them, but they let the boys live. So the king of Egypt summoned the midwives and said to them, "Why have you done this, and allowed the boys to live?" The midwives said to Pharaoh, "Because the Hebrew women are not like the Egyptian women; for they are vigorous and give birth before the midwife comes to them." So God dealt well with the midwives; and the people multiplied and became very strong. And because the midwives feared God, he gave them families (Exod. 1:15-21).

Shiphrah and Puah—hardly household names! These two brave, intensely practical women are hidden in the rich narrative of the Exodus, meriting only a few lines of text over against the exhaustive account of Moses' leadership of Israel. We are told little besides their names, but where would the story be without these midwives, tenacious and crafty guardians of new life?

Ironically, Shiphrah and Puah stand as guardians over the Exodus story and—ultimately—over *our* story. Our family album is God's word pictured by male authors and dealing primarily with male initiatives and experience, yet it is punctuated by narratives of pregnancy and birth, stories of new life that redirect and transform. Shiphrah and Puah are

*Chapter Three*
THE SPIRITUAL DIRECTOR AS MIDWIFE

joined in this album by Hagar, who fled into the wilderness with her son; Sarah, who laughed at the very idea of motherhood; Rachel, who wept for her children; and Hannah, whose fervor in prayer for a child was mistaken for drunkenness. These pivotal women of the Old Testament prepare us for *the* story, the great mystery of the Incarnation, made immediate and vivid in Luke's sensitive telling. Any woman who has carried a child within her has echoed Mary's question to the angel, "How can this be?" even as she has experienced Mary's joy, fear, and bafflement, her need for solitude and for companionship.

The language of piety is filled with the imagery of giving birth. So Paul, that reputed misogynist, describes the yearning for God in terms of the first stage of labor:

> We know that the whole creation has been groaning in labor pains until now; and not only the creation, but we ourselves, who have the first fruits of the Spirit, groan inwardly while we wait for adoption, the redemption of our bodies (Rom. 8:22-23).

Paul seems to know what he is talking about, that birth is a difficult, painful, and messy process. Most powerful of all, however, is the Gospel of John's account of Jesus' conversation with Nicodemus, the Pharisee who came to him by night, secretly and drawn by mystery (Jn. 3:1-4). Jesus answers his question before he can ask it, telling the seeker perhaps more than he wants to hear: you must be born anew. There is irony and humor in this story as two learned men discuss the logistics of birth and how to repeat a seemingly unrepeatable experience. Nicodemus, like Mary, exclaims in wonderment, "How can this be?"

The Old Testament contains a powerful image of Yahweh as a midwife. The Psalmist declares:

> Yet it was you who took me from the womb;
> you kept me safe on my mother's breast.
> On you I was cast from my birth,
> and since my mother bore me
> you have been my god. (Ps. 22:9-10).

# HOLY LISTENING
## The Art of Spiritual Direction

Set as they are in Psalm 22, that great cry of desolation and abandonment spoken by Jesus on the cross, these verses are especially poignant. We are reminded that the midwife helps new life into being and protects it; even more than the mother, she is the tender guardian of its safety. Despite decades of reading this psalm and hearing it read solemnly each Maundy Thursday, I had passed over its compelling picture of God as birth-helper until one day the words leaped at me from the page. Shiphrah and Puah may well stand as an icon, the foremothers of all midwives, but behind them is another faithful guardian of new life. The Lord is my shepherd, I shall not want. <u>The Lord is my midwife; I shall be kept safe.</u>

The maternal and birth imagery of Scripture, along with its stories of nativities both miraculous and ordinary, have become so much a part of our religious consciousness that they threaten to recede into the background like dull spiritual wallpaper. To be "born again" has a charismatic and almost disembodied ring to it; to traditional Christians it smacks of emotional excess. The Annunciation, too, has become metaphor, transformed by artists—from Hans Memling to the unnamed crafters of Christmas cards—into a beautiful tableau instead of a terrifying encounter. It helps purge the scene of sentimental piety if one is able to imagine it occurring in the ordinariness of daily life. How would I feel, I ask myself, if the angel turned up in my kitchen at the end of a long day? Or was waiting in my office when I returned, frazzled, from a class or a committee meeting? Yet these and other stories of birth and birthing are not mere background, but form the rich matrix of our faith.

One of the liberating effects of the women's movement has been to make a large amount of human experience available, acceptable, and usable. Just as Bertolt Brecht revolutionized the theater by presenting the ordinary as if it were extraordinary, so this newly broadened perspective permits new ways of seeing and of making connections. It is all too easy to see the birth imagery in Scripture (and in the lan-

## Chapter Three
## THE SPIRITUAL DIRECTOR AS MIDWIFE

guage of popular piety) as abstract, bloodless, remote from human experience. Yet if I were to name my own most profound spiritual or theological experience, without hesitation I would cite the birth of my three children. This has nothing to do with my fondness for babies as such—like everyone else they can be charming or difficult, attractive or not—nor with my personal (and biased) relationship with my own children. Rather, each birth was a glimpse into the mystery of Creation and Incarnation.

It is time that, in the words of the mystic Meister Eckhart, we attend to the new life in us. Some of us have given birth; others have witnessed or assisted in bringing babies into the world. Certainly we have all read books, seen movies, and listened to stories; all of us have our fears, revulsion, envy, and fascination with birth—and not necessarily in that order. Most important, we have all been born. We all began in the dark shelter of the womb and moved into the light. Even though we may die alone, no one was born alone, so to be born presupposes relationship, connection, and community.

Even as we are born in the human birth process, so we are born again in our baptism. If Eckhart is to be believed, we give birth and are born ourselves again and again: the birth of God in the soul is our own true birth. Like the Hebrew women in Egypt, we need help. We need midwives, those careful assistants with whom God "deals well."

The idea of the spiritual director as midwife appeals to me, for I would like to emulate Shiphrah and Puah in their courage and commitment. Or I might model my spiritual midwife on the Celtic "knee-woman" or "aid-woman," who made birth a sacrament. As described by Alexander Carmichael in his *Carmina Gadelica*, the newborn would be handed across the fire three times, then carried three times around the fire in the direction of the sun. Then the midwife continued the ritual:

> When the image of the God of life is born into the world I put three little drops of water on the child's forehead. I put the first little drop in the name of the Father, and the

watching-women say Amen. I put the second little drop in the name of the Son, and the watching-women say Amen. I put the third little drop in the name of the Spirit, and the watching-women say Amen. And I beseech the Holy Three to lave and bathe the child and to preserve it in Themselves. And the watching-women say Amen. All the people in the house are raising their voices with the watching-women, giving witness that the child has been committed to the blessed Trinity.[1]

This ritual was the "birth baptism"; the child would be formally baptized eight days later.

Most of all, I am attracted to the Appalachian granny woman of earlier days, who was willing to travel by foot or by mule over the rough terrain of the southern mountains to be present at remote and humble nativities. She lives on in oral tradition, but her image is fading. I picture her as unflappable, filled with a tough compassion, and able to make do with whatever might be at hand.

It is important to remember, though, that the midwife is not necessarily a wife, or even a woman. The literal meaning of the word is "with-woman," that is, the person who is with the birthgiver. Until recent times most women gave birth with the assistance of another woman, whose expertise was based only on her own experience of giving birth. During the nineteenth and twentieth centuries, the practice fell out of fashion and was even legally suppressed in the industrialized nations, but midwifery is now enjoying a resurgence. The new breed is neither knee women nor granny women, but highly trained health professionals.

Like the midwife, spiritual directors are with-women and with-men. While biological birthgiving is the prerogative of the female and midwives are traditionally female, in the ministry of spiritual direction, anatomy is not destiny. Accordingly, the feminine imagery and language of this chapter do not imply exclusivity. Both men and women can be sensitive midwives of the soul.

*Chapter Three*
## THE SPIRITUAL DIRECTOR AS MIDWIFE

*What the Midwife Does*

The midwife is present to another in a time of vulnerability, working in areas that are deep and intimate. It is a relationship of trust and mutual respect. Unlike most physicians, she does not fear that her professionalism will be threatened by a degree of intimacy with the women who have come to her for help. She is willing to be called by her given name, even as she addresses the birthgiver by hers. She does things *with*, not *to*, the person giving birth.

The midwife is also a teacher in the best sense of the word, in that she helps the birthgiver toward ever greater self-knowledge. At the very beginning of the relationship, she takes time to establish a comfortable rapport in which no question is irrelevant or "dumb." As the authors of *The Complete Book of Midwifery* note, "Almost every patient we've ever had in our service has told us they have felt so much more comfortable and free to be themselves with us. They are not embarrassed to ask personal questions, to expose their fears and their bodies." The midwife invites questions and then takes time to answer them: "We don't sit behind a desk and shuffle papers as we ask if a patient has any questions. We always sit down next to her and talk as long as she wants, especially during the early prenatal visits, when she's usually bursting with questions."[2]

The midwife assists at a natural event. Unlike the physician, she does not deal with sickness or pathology, but she is knowledgeable enough to seek help when these are present. She does not rely on heavy dosages of drugs to cover pain and dull memory. Traditionally, she uses her hands rather than instruments or tools. She uses them to wipe sweat from a forehead; to hold the birthgiver's hand; and finally, to guide, steady, and receive the baby. Under her guidance, the birthing is a humane process, based on sympathetic human contact throughout.

A midwife sees clearly what the birthgiver cannot see. She knows the transition period—a time of desolation, of seemingly unmanageable pain and nausea—to be a sign of breakthrough and great progress. She can encourage and interpret when the birth-giver feels she has lost control and failed. She knows when the birthgiver should push, when she should hold back, when she should breathe deeply, and when to pant in shallow breaths. The mother's body *should* know this instinctively, but fear and pain may cause her to forget.

The midwife knows how and when to confront. The art of confrontation is a delicate one, and it is sometimes mistakenly confused with a clumsy attack. To confront is quite literally to face another; in midwifery, both physical and spiritual, the helper's loving detachment can bring clarity to the situation. Sometimes it is a simple acknowledgment of the intensity of pain: "Don't be afraid to complain, even to scream. Don't be afraid to ask for relief." At other times, it is a gentle reminder that the birthgiver is still in control and has the power to help herself, so perhaps screaming is an over-dramatic and self-indulgent reaction at this point. Like a good coach or teacher or leader in combat, the midwife is able to give heart, to ask and even demand the seemingly impossible.

Finally, the midwife rejoices in the baby. With the birthgiver, she is able to celebrate the beauty and absurdity of this tiny new creature.

*The Facts of Life*

When I began to do the work of spiritual direction, and felt myself called to assist at the spiritual birthgiving of others, I was struck by its similarities to the physical birth process. For those who have not experienced the work of labor and birth first-hand, the paragraphs that follow weave together a brief sketch of the progress of pregnancy and birth along with the analogous spiritual process. (As I remind my students at the seminary, an old Red Cross film might serve the purpose equally well!)

First there is a *long period of waiting and uncertainty.* The birthgiver thinks: maybe I'm not even pregnant, but some-

*Chapter Three*
## THE SPIRITUAL DIRECTOR AS MIDWIFE

how I feel different. The range of experiences and feelings during this time is staggering—joy mingles with sadness, eager expectancy with unaccustomed drowsiness. For some there is nausea, and nearly everyone experiences the phenomenon of changing tastes—all those stale jokes about pickles and ice cream have their basis in human experience. A woman about to give birth feels as if everything were changing; emotions become extreme and unreliable. Almost simultaneously, the pregnant woman feels both helplessness and great power, hope for the future and fear of the unknown. Extraverts become introspective and amaze themselves by their bovine placidity. In time, this sense of distortion becomes physical as well as emotional: her body looks simply *wrong*, out of shape and uncomfortably tight around the waist—-at least until the pregnancy is sufficiently advanced for the proud strut of visible fecundity. And there is growing physical clumsiness—something has happened to her sense of balance!

This is a minimum list. Every time I play this game with other spiritual directors or with seminarians who are biological mothers, we are able to add to it from our collective experience. It is striking how often the same "symptoms" are displayed by those who come—either tentatively or aggressively—seeking spiritual direction.

How does a woman know she is pregnant with a child? How do you know if you are spiritually pregnant? When—on perhaps a very modest scale—the angel has come to you from the pages of Scripture, in the liturgy, in the consciousness of study or the unconsciousness of dreams? When the angel has come to you in a flash of awareness, often in a highly mundane setting—the office, the supermarket, your car on the throughway—and said, "Hail, O favored one, have I got a deal for you! Get ready to have your life turned upside down."

In both cases, time will tell. In physical pregnancy, the early signs can be deceptive, particularly for the inexperienced. Decades ago, for two months I attributed

# HOLY LISTENING
*The Art of Spiritual Direction*

mysterious and altered feelings to Mexico City's high altitude and assumed I would "adjust." Time told differently! Similarly, in later stages of pregnancy, the first flutter of new life can be dismissed as a delusion, a trick of the imagination. It simply does not seem earth-shaking enough. In the same way, the initial stirrings of the Spirit within us may be small and homely, easily discounted because they do not seem earth-shaking.

While the symptoms of spiritual malaise and imbalance bear careful attention, not everyone is "pregnant"—not everyone is a candidate for spiritual direction, at least not at every stage of life. There are those who are religiously observant and content with their spiritual lives as part of a worshipping community. It would not occur to them to enter into the intense, one-on-one relationship of traditional direction, nor even to become part of a "spiritual friends" group. This is perhaps a matter of temperament as well as generation and life experience. Then there are those whose spirituality is directed outward. They encounter God in service, in action, in outreach. Spiritual rhythms are like bodily rhythms: respiration requires both inhaling and exhaling, taking in and letting go. Frequently, but not always, those who are turning outward—exhaling, as it were—are not in the right place for spiritual direction. Later, perhaps, but not right now.

But there are those who feel that something is happening to and within them. Their tastes are changing, and their balance has shifted. Sometimes they are brought up short by a crisis: an experience of conversion, a tragic loss, a period of great pain, a sharp awareness of being on a threshold. As they approach midlife, women especially may feel impelled to explore their spirituality as they discover their new and unexpectedly authoritative voice. Men and women of all ages and life experiences may sense a call, not necessarily a vocation to the ordained ministry, but simply the awareness that God expects them to do something with their lives. What? Sometimes they merely experience a pervasive but in-

*Chapter Three*
THE SPIRITUAL DIRECTOR AS MIDWIFE

definable spiritual dis-ease which has nothing to do with pathology, but aches and itches until help is sought. Sometimes they come filled with surprise and joy: after years, perhaps decades, of faithful observance, they have experienced a sudden awareness of God's presence and grace. They feel fruitful, joyous, and expectant—and they don't know what to do about it.

As a spiritual midwife, the director's task is to pay attention, to listen to what is not being said—or to what *is* being said but minimized. Those seeking a spiritual director for the first time are almost invariably apologetic and quick to minimize their experience of annunciation, at least until they are reassured of its validity. So our conversations often begin with a disclaimer: "I'm not really sure why I'm here. I shouldn't be taking up your time. But...." Talking about God is difficult, and many of those yearning for spiritual direction lack the vocabulary to describe their symptoms and—alas!—the imagination to envision the fruit of their travail. They just know that they are experiencing inner changes, sometimes alarmingly joyful and sometimes profoundly disturbing. Spiritual distortion, imbalance, and nausea are no more pleasant than the analogous physical phenomena, even when they are signs of life and fruitfulness.

When in doubt, I always assume that God is indeed at work. It cannot be said too often: first of all, we must take each person seriously and value that person as a child of God. Just as the good host observes Benedict's admonition that each guest is to be received as if Christ himself, so the good midwife assumes that new life is germinating in the person who has sought her out.

After the long time of waiting comes the *onset of labor*. Like conversion, this can be sudden or slow and gradual. There may be some false alarms. But swift or gradual, tentative or definite, when it finally happens, there is a sense of the inevitable. There is no going back, no return to one's original state. This can be simultaneously frightening—matters are out of hand—and joyous—something is *finally* happening.

HOLY LISTENING
*The Art of Spiritual Direction*

*The First Stage: Presence, Patience, and Waiting*
Then comes *labor itself*. The terminology is apt. Birthing is hard, focused, intense work. Labor is a time of concentration, heightened awareness, and attentiveness. But it is not undifferentiated; there are distinct stages, and each must be understood and respected.

The first stage is a time of waiting for the moment of readiness. This is a time of rhythmic contractions, which grow in painful intensity. Natural childbirth enthusiasts disapprove of designating these as pains, preferring the more neutral term "contraction." But birthgiving, physical or spiritual, is not a totally upbeat process. Whether this stage is short or long, it is a time of waiting, of letting go, and breathing lightly. Above all, it is a time of receptivity and a time for patience (especially on the part of the midwife). This may go against the grain in our impatient, result-oriented society, but effort at this point is counterproductive. Similarly, while the initial stages of the direction relationship are obviously a time for story-telling, comparable to the midwife's careful taking of a medical history, much of the work of this stage is also devoted to exploring the depths of the story slowly. It is also a time to explore ways of praying, again in a gentle and unhurried way. The person who feels stuck in the printed words of the liturgy can be encouraged to pray imaginatively with Scripture, while the one who simultaneously yearns for and fears solitude might experiment with a weekend retreat at a religious house.

Spiritual direction is not a crisis ministry, even though the initial impulse to seek out a director may arise from a sense of urgent personal need. The midwife of the spirit is not an expert called in for the dramatic moments, either a crisis caused by pathology or the final, exciting moment of birth. Like a midwife, she works with the whole person and is present throughout the whole process. She "has time"—unlike the tightly scheduled physician who is concerned with specifics, complaints, and pathology. Or, for that matter, unlike the tightly scheduled parish clergy, who are concerned

*Chapter Three*
THE SPIRITUAL DIRECTOR AS MIDWIFE

with program, administration, and liturgy. Instead she offers support through every stage and waits with the birthgiver when "nothing is happening." Of course, there *are* no times when nothing is happening. Spiritual growth can be gradual and hidden; the director-midwife can discern or at least trust that something is indeed "happening."

As a people, we are not comfortable with waiting. We see it as wasted time and try to avoid it, or at least fill it with trivial busyness. We value action for its own sake. Even in retirement, people are expected to be active and boast that they are "busier than ever." It is hard to trust in the slow work of God. So the model of pregnancy and birth is a helpful one. Genetic engineers have managed in vitro fertilization, surrogate pregnancies, and astounding feats with the fecundity of milk cows—but (at least up to now!) they have not managed to speed the process of gestation. There are times when waiting is inevitable, ordained, and fruitful.

Along with our high valuation of activity itself, we believe that we can make things better by our actions. Everything can be fixed; if it isn't broken, it can be improved. One need think only of a few of our present idols: pharmacology, medical technology, psychotherapy, and political and economic systems of the right and of the left. Yet much of spiritual direction is in the company of those who are waiting, who cannot be fixed, repaired, or made right, and the spiritual director does well to emulate the midwife's restraint. The midwife understands the process of birthing. At least in the old days, she had experienced it as well. She knows when she can assist and interpret and when she should merely be present. She intervenes only when necessary and helpful, never for the sake of "doing something."

In spiritual directors as in others, the urge to "help" people dies hard. Even when the director thinks himself purged of such naiveté, the impulse creeps back in, often in ever more subtle forms. This is especially true when someone is in genuine distress and when it is obvious that remediable outward circumstances are affecting her spiritual life. People

# HOLY LISTENING
*The Art of Spiritual Direction*

come to us with what seem like crushing burdens: chronic illness, both physical and emotional, poverty, the scars of physical abuse. To the director, such conditions may seem like adverse ones to be got rid of, or at least tidied up, and it is a hard lesson that life in Christ is not necessarily a life free from pain.

One woman I see, Jennie, is isolated, chronically ill, facing ever greater impairment, and living at the edge of poverty. Not long ago as we sat together, I found myself thinking, "If only this woman had a little more money, everything would change. Sure, she would still be ill and lonely, but...." I felt myself getting caught in plans to "help" her, to point out ways of "fixing everything." Finally, I blurted out, "I want to take away your pain. I want to be able to make all this go away." Jennie looked at me with infinite patience, patted my hand, and said, "Honey, just knowing that you're there and that you love me is enough. Don't worry about it." She knew what I had forgotten: that sometimes one waits because there is nothing else to be done. The greatest gift I could give her was not to play social worker or psychotherapist, but to quiet down and wait with her. Be with her. To do this, I had to recognize my discomfort at my own powerlessness.

Just as we are not comfortable with waiting, we shrink from passivity, from being the object rather than the initiator of action. The most minor illness can reveal the fragility of our control, as it turns us into *patients*, those who are recipients of the actions of others, be they healing or hurtful. When we are patients, we have either relinquished control or been deprived of it, an offensive condition. Even ascetical theologians would rather talk about it than experience it. We may play a bit at an Eckhartian detachment, letting go of those habits or ways of being that are easy to give up, but praying to be spared the cataclysmic experience that rips our carefully woven (or patched!) fabric to shreds. Yet the model of holy waiting, of passivity, is before us in the life of Christ.

In his wise book, *The Stature of Waiting*, W. H. Vanstone points out the radical change in Jesus from action to passion,

*Chapter Three*
THE SPIRITUAL DIRECTOR AS MIDWIFE

noting that the term "passion" refers not so much to his suffering as to his being "done unto," becoming the object rather than the subject of the action. In Mark's gospel, after Judas "hands him over" (Vanstone prefers this to the more usual translation "betrays"), Jesus is inactive, speaks very little and then ineffectively. In John's gospel, with the coming of night, he becomes inactive. No work can be done at night; it is the time for waiting.

> In John's Gospel, at the moment when Jesus is arrested in the Garden, He is bound there and then....[His] unfettered freedom is suddenly changed for bondage, His impalpability to human hands for the literal and physical hold of those hands upon Him. At the moment when Jesus is handed over He passes, according to John, from unfettered freedom to total constraint.[3]

In our Faustian culture, which values doing over being, it is illuminating to read either Mark's or John's gospel with Vanstone's eyes. To wait is part of the human condition. But instead of being a regrettable yet inevitable waste, it is a condition for growth, potentially holy and even Christlike. As Vanstone reminds us, "Waiting can be the most intense and poignant of all human experiences—the experience which, above all others, strips us of affectation and self-deception and reveals to us the reality of our needs, our values, and ourselves."[4] As midwives of the spirit, we will do a great deal of waiting and encourage others to wait, not always in comfort and sometimes in great pain.

Those who are graced with insight are able to glimpse their essential powerlessness, even though outwardly they are achievers who contribute by their diligence to the common wellbeing. (Teresa of Avila is an outstanding example.) These are the people who often come to us for spiritual direction, baffled by the realization of the emptiness of their busy lives and frightened by the awareness of their essential impotence. They want to push hard at life, even as they see that this is only making the pain worse and delaying fruition. As

HOLY LISTENING
*The Art of Spiritual Direction*

midwives, we invite them to embrace the passivity of waiting, to breathe lightly and become receptive.

This is not as easy as it sounds. I realize that when I meet with Charles, a successful pastor who lives at the edge of burnout. The spiritual and financial vigor of his parish is the envy of his colleagues, his parishioners turn to him with love and respect bordering on veneration, and his bishop thinks of him first when looking for a diocesan committee chairman. Yet Charles finds his life gray and empty. He wonders why he is working so hard, since nothing seems to matter. He wonders why he continues to pray, since that too no longer seems to matter. We both know that he is in a waiting place, but the waiting is hard: Charles is not a man to breathe lightly and stop pushing! Yet his faith is deep, and his trust sufficient. He is willing to hang on. My only task, at this point, is to hang on with him.

Others come who are outwardly as well as spiritually in a waiting place. The frail aged, the physically immobile, and the chronically ill are obvious examples. Presence is one of our greatest gifts to the dying, whose loved ones and caregivers frequently discourage them from talking about their experiences. The spiritual director can wait and listen, accepting with the dying person the fact of death. We wait too with the bereaved, knowing that grief cannot be hurried but must be lived through. We sit with victims of all kinds, including the survivors of violence, abuse, and neglect.

Spiritual directors also have a ministry of presence to the unemployed, whose plight is seen in economic or social terms but seldom recognized as a spiritual crisis. Similarly, retired persons, although their retirement may be voluntary and welcome, find themselves passive, "done unto," even in the midst of pleasurable activities. Rather than offering more activities to mask reality, the spiritual director can model an acceptance of waiting and invite exploration of its holy emptiness. In less traditional settings, our ministry to the homeless and the imprisoned is also a ministry of patient and attentive waiting.

*Chapter Three*
## THE SPIRITUAL DIRECTOR AS MIDWIFE

I realize that these paragraphs may sound like a prescription for benign neglect of those who—materially or physically—have been "given over" and find themselves dependent on the actions of others. Nothing could be farther from the truth. Spiritual directors are not social workers, however, nor are they physicians or community planners. We cannot and should not try to replace the professionals, programs, and agencies that work to alleviate suffering and promote individual and community wholeness. But we can offer what is inevitably absent from the best-intentioned activism: a willingness to wait with others in the face of their powerlessness, "to sit still, even amid these rocks."[5]

### Mutual Presence

In her attentive presence, the midwife is not authoritarian, yet she has great authority. She has skill, knowledge, and perspective that the birthgiver cannot have, if only because she stands outside the process. She is capable of a loving detachment, but at the same time feels solidarity with the one giving birth. The midwife of the spirit, too, needs to experience such solidarity. In her perceptive book on women and spiritual direction, Kathleen Fischer notes that the myth of the expert is more harmful to women than it is to men, since women have been conditioned to rely on authority. Hence she urges the demystification of the process of spiritual guidance and cautions especially against patterning the relationship on a scientific model with its emphasis on distance and objectivity, which are not suitable for healing and personal growth.[6] In other words, even the highly skilled spiritual midwife retains the openness and the emotional involvement of the amateur. The loving detachment of the spiritual midwife is not synonymous with distance. While the authority of the midwife is a welcome support to the one giving birth, she is engaged and emotionally involved, even in her detachment. It cannot be said too often: she is not afraid to be touched.

HOLY LISTENING
*The Art of Spiritual Direction*

With the clearer perspective of the midwife who stands outside the process, the spiritual director is able to offer interpretations to the birthgiver. I say "offer" rather than "impose," for the director-midwife can never see the whole picture. Perhaps the directee is unwilling or unable to disclose some essential part of the story, or the director's insight is offered prematurely. This is a time for humility and patience on the part of the director, who may fear that a tentative approach lacks strength. Then, too, both people may be growing uncomfortable with the uncertainty of waiting and yearn for clarity, even if it is premature and mistaken. For most of us, loose ends are frightening reminders of our own powerlessness. To name, to label, to classify gives us the illusion of control, even if the closure reached is a false one.

In any event, it is important to leave the directee free to accept or reject our insights. Whether we are right, wrong, or premature, it is also reassuring to remember that we cannot do too much harm since people rarely hear what they are not ready to hear. At the very least, we may have planted a seed. As director-midwives, we then must be willing to wait for the seed to sprout and grow to maturity, perhaps long after our relationship with the directee has ceased.

While we leave the directee to accept or reject our interpretations, we can help simply by saying the words, since there is truth in the cliché that demons are destroyed when they are named. At the same time, we can help liberate the directee from the tyranny of "shoulds" and "oughts." Even if the director is wise enough to avoid prescribing behavior, the directee may be self-imprisoned. So we hear, "I shouldn't feel this way, but..." or "I ought not to say this, but..." The place of waiting is not necessarily a place of slavish unfreedom nor of repressive denial. The director can gently or briskly clear the air. I find myself saying, "But you *do* feel this way," or "Who's going to be offended if you go ahead and say it anyway? God already knows about it, and I probably won't fall off my chair."

*Chapter Three*
## THE SPIRITUAL DIRECTOR AS MIDWIFE

As we wait together in spiritual direction, we are not altogether sure what we are waiting *for*. Eckhart presents us with the image of a God so filled with love that he is repeatedly born in the empty, welcoming space of the soul. With the sadness and resignation of our own time, philosopher Jacob Needleman, author of numerous books on the spiritual search, sounds like a pessimistic Eckhart when he notes that the soul is aborted a thousand times a day.[7] But whether we rejoice with Eckhart in his vision of abundant fecundity or whether we grieve with Needleman at lost promise and wasted life, it is clear that for spiritual directors even seeming emptiness is not sterile. In the times of waiting, it is enough if we do nothing more than sit with the birthgiver, offering a hand to be held.

The midwife's comforting hand is welcome, for it is a prevailing fear of laboring women that they will be left alone. More accurately, abandonment is the fear of us all, although with the passing of infancy we learn to control or at least conceal it. As I listen to the stories of my directees, it strikes me that we all feel abandoned and that we expend great (and frequently misplaced) energy trying to deal with our grief and rage at parental desertion. Misplaced, because we do not tap deep enough for the roots of our fear: that we will be abandoned by God.

Thus George is reluctant to explore his relationship with either a loving or neglectful God, insisting that God is not the problem, but his cold and abandoning father. His father no doubt *was* cold and abandoning forty-five years ago, but now he is ancient and semi-disabled. While George bears scars and slowly healing wounds—who doesn't?—he is a man of considerable gifts. He resists my suggestion that he seek psychotherapy to gain insight into his relationship with his father, who serves a useful purpose as both a screen and diversion to keep George from facing his deeper fear. The God whom he has created and keeps on a shelf is beneficent, albeit rather ineffectual, and not nearly so powerful—or so absorbing—as Daddy. Perhaps someday George will feel strong enough to put his father aside, if not to forgive him, and look squarely at his relationship with a God of love and terror. Perhaps with the Psalmist he will then be able to pray: "How long, O Lord? will you forget me forever? how long will you hide your face from me? How long shall I have perplexity in my mind, and grief in my heart, day after day?" A great barrier will then be broken, and a frozen place in George will begin to melt. I am not sure, however, that this can happen unless he is willing to seek professional help to heal the injuries he carries within him. At present, he is not ready to give them up.

Not all directees present themselves in George's stark terms, but many share his reluctance to articulate their sense of abandonment by God. Here, as elsewhere, they are quick to blame themselves and suppress any feelings of anger. If they feel cut off, they must have done something to deserve it. The director can help here by reminding them that their experience is not unique, not in a way that seeks to minimize their pain but rather to diminish their isolation.

*Transition*

The first stage of labor ends in a period of transition, which can be frightening, even terrifying if it is unexpected. Even when the transition it is understood, it is of surprising power. The birthgiver is gripped by tremendous force and feels that she has somehow lost control. Everything is suddenly too big and too powerful. All the weeks of careful preparation and instruction seem inadequate and trivial. The birthgiver had thought she was prepared and "knew just what to do"—and now it doesn't work! She might even feel betrayed: no one has told her the truth, or perhaps no one has previously confronted and understood the truth.

In the birth process, the dark, seemingly chaotic period of transition is the time of greatest discomfort and—at least from the birthgiver's viewpoint—greatest need for the supportive presence of the midwife. In our spiritual lives, too, it is a pivotal time. The old ways no longer serve. The comfort-

*Chapter Three*
THE SPIRITUAL DIRECTOR AS MIDWIFE

able rhythms of worship and solitary prayer feel empty and sterile. Gone is the image of a loving, immanent God, the God who asks:

> Can a woman forget her nursing child, or show no compassion for the child of her womb? Even these may forget, yet I will not forget you. See I have inscribed you on the palms of my hands... (Isa. 49:15-16).

This vision may have been supplanted by the forbidding image of an angry, punitive God:

> Who can stand before his indignation? Who can endure the heat of his anger? His wrath is poured out like fire, and by him the rocks are broken in pieces (Nah. 1:6).

Even more likely is the perception of the absence or indifference of God, a God who chooses to stand aside:

> Why, O Lord, do you stand far off?
> Why do you hide yourself in
> time of trouble? (Ps. 10:1)

What has been learned and diligently practiced no longer helps. Nothing is going the way it should, or at least the way we expect it to go. The lonely times of transition can be terrible, for they are times of spiritual homelessness. Although neither a midwife nor a spiritual director (yet perhaps a little of both), the poet Rilke offers a moving description of this uncomfortable yet fruitful stage of transition when he speaks of

> moments when something new has entered into us, something unknown; our feelings grow mute in shy perplexity, everything in us withdraws, a stillness comes, and the new, which no one knows, stands in the midst of it and is silent....I believe that almost all our sadnesses are moments of tension that we find paralyzing because we no longer hear our surprised feelings living. Because we are alone with the alien thing that has entered our self; because everything intimate and accustomed is for an instant taken away; because we stand in the middle of a transition where we cannot remain standing.[8]

# HOLY LISTENING
*The Art of Spiritual Direction*

Not surprisingly, transitions are a time when people whose religious observance has heretofore been tepid and perfunctory are impelled seek spiritual direction. Others, if they are well established in a relationship of spiritual direction, may decide to leave it during a period of transition because they feel that it is somehow "not working." Or they may sense that they are poised on the brink of something new, and they are reluctant to take the next step. The woman described in Chapter Two, who left spiritual direction because it was too costly, was exceptionally self-aware and candid. More commonly, the resistance to change is unconscious and unarticulated. In all cases, however, it is the director's task to discern where the directee is, despite confusing and conflicting signals, and to be aware of both the pain and the promise of transition.

Transitions may be big or small, welcome or unwelcome. Sometimes they can be anticipated, but often they come as a surprise. The obvious ones involve painful loss—death of a loved one, major illness, divorce or other broken relationships, and unemployment. Retirement or other drastic changes in manner or place of living are also obvious times of transition. Sometimes the transitions are triggered by positive and welcome changes in the directee's life: the beginning of sobriety, acceptance of one's sexual orientation after a long period of struggle, marriage, the birth of a child, resolution of vocational questions. Instead of the expected smooth sailing, the directee experiences spiritual chaos; everything seems to break down just at the time that he "has it all together."

Even when there are no outward triggering events, an apparent loss of faith may signal a time of transition. This is a common experience of seminarians, who find their faith shaken just when they expect it to be firmest, and academic studies do not assuage the pain as they are forced to look critically at Scripture and history. Similarly, women may find themselves adrift, with all sense of order and meaning taken from them, when they suddenly (or gradually) find themselves cut off by the masculine language of the liturgy. In an

*Chapter Three*
THE SPIRITUAL DIRECTOR AS MIDWIFE

essay called "Take Back the Night," Mary E. Giles describes this painful time of liminality:

> In countless situations today women are undergoing the loss of traditional values, systems and relationships to the distress of themselves and their loved ones and to the dismay of those in institutions affected by their experience. When the loss is radical, that is, when it affects our total being, is unplanned and unwanted, reduces us to emotional, intellectual and physical helplessness, leaves us suspended between a darkened past and a dark future so that all of our being rails against the loss, then we are undergoing our dark night. When we cry in anguish 'God, my God,' when we feel empty of all meaning, when we do not know who this God is to whom we dumbly cling, then we are undergoing our dark night. No hint of exotic adventure here, just groping and grasping.[9]

In either case, faithful people find themselves in a situation where the old ways no longer serve and from which they cannot retreat. They may be tempted to carry on as if nothing has happened, especially if circumstances encourage conformity. Most seminarians, for example, would wisely refrain from discussing their painful and difficult state with the screening bodies who approve them for ordination. In the safety of the spiritual direction relationship, however, they can live through this stage in candor and even come to see its necessity.

The director can help by naming the transition for what it is: a time of movement from one stage to another, a time of change and transformation. With Rilke, we can counsel that this is a time to be "still, patient, and open."[10] Even the theologically sophisticated directee can be helped by the reminder that our images of God are just that—images—and as we see their limitations, we outgrow them. The difficulty comes when we forget that they are merely images and think instead we have outgrown God. The spiritually stagnant are able to live in a state of denial, but the seeker after God may panic: "Perhaps I have gone too far! I should have been content with the God I had!" At its very best, this is an unsettling place to be. The ground no longer feels firm beneath one's feet and, as one of my down-to-earth directees says, "Everything is up for grabs."

As a faithful midwife, the director can see patterns and form in seeming formlessness. More importantly, he knows that the time of transition has a beginning and an end, and that the directee will emerge from it into a new level of clarity. This is a time to share his insights with the directee, who may be sceptical but should have sufficient trust to know that these are not words of cheap consolation. Even directees who have not experienced birthgiving are able to understand the imagery of transition as a difficult and confusing stage leading to new life. It remains difficult, but they sense a meaning in its apparent meaninglessness. The midwife-director can help them to let go, to cease to struggle, and to watch attentively for the beginning of the next stage. Transition is a time of surprises; the director can help by pointing out signs in unexpected places.

One of the unwelcome surprises of transition is the sense of loss that inevitably accompanies self-transcendence and new growth. Thus new parents are often surprised by the losses experienced in the birth of a much-wanted child: spontaneity, privacy, self-determination, even loss of a sense of identity. To a growing number of people, they are now merely somebody's parents. To accept growth and change in oneself is also a kind of departure, a leaving behind of the safe and the known. Sometimes we realize the poignancy of our loss only after the fact, but there is no returning home.

One of the treasures in my study is the intact skin of a Virginia black snake, shed as part of the process of growth. To grow, indeed to survive, that snake had to leave behind a part of itself. I have no idea whether the shedding was painful or a relief, but my imagination tells me that it was some of each. Directees, too, shed skins and identities if they persevere through the pain of transitions, giving up the safety of an outworn images and habits to embrace the new. This is especially poignant since there is often "nothing wrong"

*Chapter Three*
## THE SPIRITUAL DIRECTOR AS MIDWIFE

with the old identity or shed skin; it is simply not useful anymore.

### The Second Stage: Active Work

The second stage begins in the midst of the chaos of transition, with an instinctive awareness of the need to push hard with each contraction. This is the time of active work—as contrasted with the work of waiting. All the birthgiver's attention is concentrated, focused, and centered, which brings with it excitement, relief, and great energy. (This might, however, not be apparent to the casual observer, who expects to see signs of pain and exhaustion.)

For the spiritual midwife, this second stage is harvest time. The relationship with the directee is well established, with affection and trust on both sides. The long period of waiting is past, and the bleakness of transition has been lived through.

The director may feel that his presence is less important for now, for more than ever, the directee is leading the way. This is a good time to remember again what spiritual direction really is. It is not imposing one's will on another, but respectfully assisting as the path is discerned: which way do I go? what are the signs? which turn should I take? what is my direction?

At this stage—and it is important to remember that this is not final, that the whole process will start over again and again—the direction is clear, the energy level is high, and the next steps are apparent. For now, the directee has found the rule and discipline that is right for her. For the present moment, at least, she knows who she is, with a new awareness of her identity in Christ. At this time of hard but focused work, the directee lives into that identity and lives out the insights gained in the earlier stages. It is always clear to me when I work with seminarians that spiritual direction is linked with concern for vocation, for the outer and inner paths are inextricably tangled. Less obviously, all those who seek us out are wrestling with vocation, regardless of their

# HOLY LISTENING
*The Art of Spiritual Direction*

daily occupations. So in a sense, spiritual direction can be seen as vocational guidance—bearing, I hope, little resemblance to the course many of us endured in high school!

This stage of labor is not without its own pain. As the inner work progresses, the directee experiences ever greater awareness both of herself and also of all creation. What may have started as a voyage of self-discovery becomes a journey into the great web of connection. Compassion deepens as the directee grows beyond self-absorption, and compassion is never a cheap or easy gift. What has been seen cannot be unseen; what is known can not be unknown. Giving birth is not without its dark side: the inevitable changes may be more than the directee has bargained for.

As it is so often, the director's task here is to encourage, quite literally, to give heart. In this stage I feel like a coach: you're on the right path, don't stop now, keep going, trust yourself! Don't forget to watch for signs! And don't be surprised at surprises! This is the time when friendship becomes a stronger component in the relationship. It has been there all along, but now the directee knows what the director has known from the beginning: both of us on the same path and doing the same work. The barriers between us are flimsy structures, erected for convenience, or perhaps they are completely illusory.

We do not come to this point quickly, but I always find it rewarding. The directee who may have begun our work together with an exaggerated idea of my competence is now willing to see me in my flawed humanity and still love me. After all, he has been doing all the work!

*Celebration*

It is impossible to describe the joy that fills the room at the birth of the child. A midwife friend tells me that the excitement of welcoming new life never grows old. I wept and laughed simultaneously at the first sight of each of my children—beautiful, yet so small, and even to my favorably

*Chapter Three*
## THE SPIRITUAL DIRECTOR AS MIDWIFE

prejudiced eye, slightly comic. All the waiting and work had brought forth this morsel of promise. There is both mystery and absurdity in raw new life, and only those who have not seen it in its newness and rawness can indulge in sentimental and romantic rhapsodies about it. A helpless little creature, dusky purple and rather bizarre, is the fruit of all this waiting, pain, terror, and hard work. Surely something more handsome and useful might be expected!

We can often make such heavy work of spiritual direction that we may forget to celebrate. People find it so easy to say negative things about themselves that it is possible to overlook all the small births, the times for joy and celebration. Sometimes I wonder what passersby must think when they see my solemn "Do Not Disturb" sign on the door and hear laughter coming from within. Surely a spiritual direction meeting is a solemn if not lugubrious occasion for listing faults and uncovering deficiencies. Yet it is self-absorption that leads us to forget the gracious love of God, the giver of new life in the most tired and wounded soul. Even though it is intensely serious, spiritual direction will be an occasion for celebration. Eckhart was right when he said, "Tend only to the birth in you and you will find all goodness and all consolation, all delight, all being and all truth. Reject it and you reject goodness and blessing. What comes to you in this birth brings with it pure being and blessing."

Not everyone who comes to work with us will be John of the Cross or Teresa of Avila. Most of the people who come to us will be ordinary folk, not candidates for sanctity. Some will bear deep emotional wounds; all will be scarred to some extent. Most of them won't be theologians, and they may be notably lacking in self-confidence. But as we work together, they will bring forth new life—almost always small and helpless and slightly comic, but at the same time mysterious and holy. It is time for rejoicing and celebration, even when the midwife knows that this is just the beginning, the first of many births. Sooner or later, the whole process must begin again.

# Endnotes

1  Quoted in *The Celtic Vision*, Esther de Waal, ed. (Petersham, MA: St. Bede's, 1988), p. 111. A similar prayer is recorded by Avery Brooke in *Celtic Prayers* (New York: Seabury, 1981), pp. 22-27.

2  Barbara Brennan and Joan Rattner Heilman, *The Complete Book of Midwifery* (New York: E. P. Dutton, 1977).

3  W. H. Vanstone, *The Stature of Waiting* (New York: Seabury, 1983), p. 27.

4  *Ibid.*, p. 83.

5  T. S. Eliot, "Ash Wednesday," in *Collected Poems* (New York: Harcourt Brace and Company, 1936), p. 121.

6  Kathleen Fischer, *Women at the Well: Feminist Perspectives in Spiritual Direction* (New York: Paulist, 1988), pp. 19-20.

7  Jacob Needleman, *Lost Christianity: A Journey of Rediscovery* (San Francisco: Harper & Row, 1980), p. 175.

8  Rilke, *Letters*, p. 64.

9  Mary E. Giles, ed., *The Feminist Mystic and Other Essays on Women and Spirituality* (New York: Crossroad, 1989), pp. 61-62.

10  Rilke, *Letters*, p. 65.

CHAPTER FOUR

# Women and Spiritual Direction

Jesus said to her, Mary. First he had called her "Woman," the common address at that time for one of her sex, without being recognized. Then he called her by her own name, as if to say: "Recognize him who recognizes you."

*Gregory the Great*


"Everyone who drinks of this water will be thirsty again, but those who drink of the water that I will give them will never be thirsty. The water that I give will become in them a spring of water gushing up to eternal life." The woman said to him, "Sir, give me this water, so that I may never be thirsty."

*John 4:13-15*

# Women and Spiritual Direction

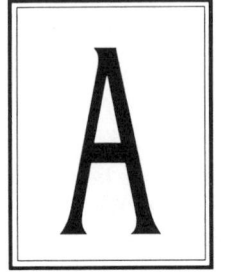

Although there is growing awareness that women's spirituality is distinctive, it has until recently been largely unexplored. What is perhaps the seminal work in the investigation of women's spirituality was written by an academic psychologist rather than a theologian and intended for a lay readership: Carol Gilligan's *In a Different Voice* offered a fresh vision of women as moral decision-makers. For me and many of my friends, this was an "aha!" book: we saw ourselves in it, and behold, it was very good. Mary Field Belenky and her collaborators have provided a valuable study in *Women's Ways of Knowing,* doing for epistemology what Gilligan had done for ethics: not only do women judge differently, they learn differently. Now works by women about women's spirituality proliferate, although there is a lot of catching up to be done, and the valuable work of such writers as Joann Wolski Conn, Kathleen Fischer, Madonna Kolbenschlag, and Sandra Schneiders are only the beginning.

From working with many male colleagues and reading their books, I am convinced that women function differently as directors—not better, not worse, but differently. They bring special gifts, a unique perspective, and their vulnerabilities. From spending thousands of hours with women who are directees, I am convinced that they too bring special gifts, perspectives, and vulnerabilities to the practice of spiritual direction. It would be a great loss, however, if this increased awareness of the distinctive qualities of women's spirituality led to some kind of rigid separatism. As men and

*Chapter Four*
## WOMEN AND SPIRITUAL DIRECTION

women, we are completed by each other; this is as true in the spiritual direction relationship as in any other. There are times when women work most fruitfully and honestly with other woman, and times when the "otherness" of a male director is beneficial for women.

Most women know the stories and language of men. Just as I learned in graduate school to function well in a context and terminology that was not my own, most women know the accepted language of religious observance and traditional spirituality. Yet we cannot expect openness and sensitivity from men until they are equally acquainted with the spirituality and language of women. Some male directors may persist in an unconscious but arrogant assumption that their language, perceptions, and experience are the norm, and women who turn to them for spiritual direction will be patronized or dismissed outright. Fortunately, however, a growing number of men are becoming aware of the differences—the differences of language, life experience, experience of God, ways of praying, and ways of sinning. Their eagerness to know and to understand is a great step toward wholeness and reconciliation in the church.

In the pages that follow, I will reflect first about women as spiritual directors: how their way of working differs from that of their male colleagues, what their special gifts might be, and what their limitations are. Then I will turn to my first-hand experience of women as directees and the special needs and strengths women bring to this relationship.

### Women as Listeners

As a member of my seminary's admissions committee, I interview many prospective students and frequently meet with people in the very early stages of exploring a vocation to the priesthood. Again and again I am struck by the number of women—of all ages, levels of education, and professional experience—who are drawn to some kind of listening ministry. They can easily envision themselves as chaplains in hospitals, hospices, schools, and prisons. They may need supervision to help understand their own motives, but upon admission to seminary these same women perform superbly in the practical and pastoral parts of their training. However impatient they may become with systematic theology or clumsy with scriptural exegesis, their gifts as listeners are beyond question.

Such gifts are deeply inbred, and they carry with them the potential for misuse. Traditionally, female children have been socialized to "be there for others," which includes attentiveness, listening. At least during certain stages in a woman's developing self-awareness, this careful listening is a valid way to learn about herself. So the motive is less altruistic than it might appear: in addition to the satisfaction of being "generous" and "good," which are questionable motives for the mature spiritual director, the woman is achieving something important to her own development. As the authors of *Women's Ways of Knowing* observe,

> Women typically approach adulthood with the understanding that the care and empowerment of others is central to their life's work. Through listening and responding, they draw out the voices and minds of those they help to raise up. In the process, they often come to hear, value and strengthen their own voices and minds as well.[1]

Such a role is safe for women, for they need reveal little of themselves as they listen. Since she is primarily interested in taking in and absorbing from the speaker, a woman will appear—and indeed be—free of judgment, so others are drawn to her and trust her.

I am convinced that many women feel the call to a listening ministry, be it a chaplaincy or spiritual direction, when they find others turning to them and trusting them in this way. Even when it meets unconscious needs, the call to ministry is often a valid one. At this point, the sought-after listener is by no means a spiritual director; if she thinks she is, she risks pretentiousness and self-deception. But her gifts at listening as an unconscious means of self-understanding can be a fruitful first step toward ministry, as she grows to a suf-

*Chapter Four*
WOMEN AND SPIRITUAL DIRECTION

ficiently secure sense of self to be able to put that self aside. She no longer needs to *use* others to learn about herself, although increasing self-knowledge is an inevitable concomitant of doing spiritual direction. Rather, she can employ her highly developed listening skills in a spirit of loving detachment. She can listen *maternally.*

I am indebted to the authors of *Women's Ways of Knowing* for the concept of maternal listening and, more broadly, maternal conversation. Their studies indicate that women tend to talk about personal matters with their mothers and impersonal matters with their fathers. When they do happen to discuss personal topics with their fathers, these men tell their daughters what they ought to do.

> That such differences between mothers and fathers are so common may be accounted for by the fact that many men are used to being the expert, while many women are used to consulting others; many men are interested in how experience is generalized and universalized, while many women are interested in what can be learned from the particular....[2]

The authors emphasize that this is not a sign of greater caring on the part of the mother or coldness in the father. Rather, the mother tries to help on the daughter's terms, while the father's help is offered on his terms.

Maternal conversation is an appropriate mode for spiritual direction. The director is willing to listen and to be present to the directee where he is. By the very nature of the relationship, the director has been given tacit permission to ask questions. (This is in contrast to polite conversation, which forbids asking anything that really matters.) But they must be the right questions, asked in a spirit of attentive love. In her essay on "Forms of the Implicit Love of God," Simone Weil writes compellingly of this generous and compassionate attentiveness as manifested in the story of the Good Samaritan:

> Christ taught us that the supernatural love of our neighbor is the exchange of compassion and gratitude which hap-

pens in a flash between two beings, one possessing and the other deprived of human personality. One of the two is only a little piece of flesh, naked, inert, and bleeding beside a ditch; he is nameless, no one knows anything about him. Those who pass by scarcely notice it....Only one stops and turns his attention toward it. The actions that follow are just the automatic effect of this moment of attention. The attention is creative.[3]

While the people who come to us for spiritual direction are rarely in such dire straits as the injured man in the parable, by our own attentive love we can help them toward wholeness. As the authors of *Women's Ways of Knowing* observe, "It is through attentive love, the ability to ask, 'What are you going through?' and the ability to hear the answer that the reality of the child is both created and respected."[4] The questions are not a means of amassing data; rather, they are open-ended and compassionate, an invitation to trust. The director must be willing to hear the answer and resist the temptation to offer glib advice.

Even the experienced director should not lose sight of the perils that accompany his or her gifts as a listener. It is gratifying to be trusted and heady to be relied upon. Human life and lives are infinitely fascinating; and, unless the director works out of a satisfying context of personal relationships, there is the danger of becoming a spiritual voyeur, of using and feeding upon the other. My inner alarm bells sound when I find myself growing curious, taking sides, or becoming over-invested emotionally. I know that I am about to step over an invisible line and that the delicate balance can be destroyed. Even if my words and actions remain correct, I am in danger of using the directee for my own gratification.

## Women as Outsiders

Over the centuries, women have kept the church going by their faithfulness, but have lived their inner lives around its edges. One of my less reverent fantasies about the Last Supper includes some women in the kitchen, their faces rosy with the heat of the oven, peeping through the pass-through

*Chapter Four*
WOMEN AND SPIRITUAL DIRECTION

to watch and eavesdrop, perhaps to be awarded with a word of praise and spatter of applause for the excellent roast lamb. They are included, yet there is always a "Yes, but...." The old myth of uncleanness is now in poor taste, but it lingers on in woman's otherness, which—up to now—the church has not been able to incorporate.

Not surprisingly, the idea that women might be spiritual guides gains slow acceptance. Yet it is frequently their very otherness that makes them able and open as spiritual directors, especially effective in ministry on the margins and in the cracks. Their own experience enables them to work well with the disaffected, those who do not trust the institutional church even though they are drawn to it. Most particularly, they are accessible to other women, both the gently despairing and the victims of abuse. When the directee is burdened by shame, she may feel safest with another women, particularly a laywoman. And the director will hear again and again, "I just couldn't talk to Father about this. It's embarrassing, and I know it's not very spiritual, but...."

Sandra Schneiders has written perceptively about the special quality of women's ministry, resulting from their centuries-long exclusion from the inner circles. Having never been "ritualized," their ministry is often unrecognized and unnamed, but nevertheless powerful because it has had to be personalized. She observes that "it belongs to the very nature of ritual that it largely subsumes the individuality of the ritualist. Women's ministry has never been anything other than the personal service of one human being to another in the name of Christ."[5] His ministry provides the model for the director who is "other" and most at home at the margins and in the crevices. Schneiders goes on to point out that

> the nonritualized ministry of women has contributed very little to the pervasive image of the Christian God as a stern, even violent, father-figure bent on exact justice and retribution. Indeed, experienced spiritual directors know that, when a person's violent God-image begins to be healed, that healing is often effected by, and expressed in, a recog-

nition in God of the qualities one has experienced in the women in one's life—mother, sister, wife, or lover.[6]

The marginality and powerlessness of a woman spiritual director gives her great freedom. She can be open to all sorts and conditions of men and women, with no need to condemn or exclude because some official standard is not met. This makes her sensitive to the stories and experience of those whom society has pushed to the edges or tried to render invisible—the frail aged, the abused, gay men, and lesbians.

What will happen as more women's voices are heard, as women move from the edges toward the center, as they become equal partners in the establishment? Will the church change and grow toward wholeness because of their inclusion, or will women lose their spiritual freedom as they lose their marginality? In the meantime, they must still work to be taken seriously—especially lay women, whose gifts in spiritual direction are often unrecognized or undervalued. It is easier for directors who are ordained or are members of a religious order: a clerical collar or a religious habit makes a statement of authority. While academic courses or an impressive certificate cannot form a director when the innate gift is not there, seminary study, programs of certification, or a unit of Clinical Pastoral Education can set a woman director free to acknowledge and claim her authority. This is not to minimize the importance of formal study or supervised work, but the chief value of training is to legitimize this ministry in a time obsessed with credentials.

*Women as Nurturers*

While Jesus is our primary model for the spiritual director as teacher, there are others, and it is easy to overlook his first teacher: his mother. Like all infants, Jesus learned about being human from looking into her face, hearing her voice, feeling her touch. She was the first person to teach him about steadfast love. From her, he learned about feeding, washing, and healing—surely women's work, yet an essential part of

*Chapter Four*
WOMEN AND SPIRITUAL DIRECTION

his ministry. Even as the scholars in the temple taught the twelve-year-old of the abstract, unknowable God, so did his mother provide a base in physical, human experience.

This awareness helps me in spiritual direction because it keeps before me the unquestioning and tenacious love of mothers. Even with the example of Mary, the desert ammas, and Julian of Norwich before me, however, I approach the idea of the maternal spiritual director with trepidation. Surely spiritual directors are not expected to infantilize those who turn to them, or to smother them with affection, for such behavior is not good mothering. Good mothering enables the child to develop his own capabilities, grow to maturity, and move away from reliance on the mother. My Virginia neighbors, the black bears, are competent mothers: the cubs are nurtured as long as necessary and then sent briskly on their way. The mother bears may be lacking in tenderness, but they understand their role!

While I haven't yet reached this state of detachment, I have spent too long with the day-to-day realities of mothering to be sentimental about it. If I am now perceived as a motherly person, I would prefer to be seen as a desert amma rather than a Hallmark mommy. Most important, for good or ill, I know that my own experience in mothering colors the way in which I do spiritual direction. And lest it sound as if I am excluding a large segment of the population, Meister Eckhart reminds us that we can all be mothers. While the experience of bearing and nurturing a child is unique, maternal ways of being are available to all of us, men and women.

Being a mother calls for a great deal of patience. The whole process begins with a long wait. Then, even after the child is born, he develops slowly. Simply holding up his head is a major achievement, and it is hard for the mother to realize that this small creature will one day become mobile, acquire speech, and understand computers. Each small step toward maturity and self-sufficiency is cause for rejoicing. The wise mother knows the stages of development and never expects the impossible, so she is able to put her own needs aside and meet the child where he is. In biological motherhood, this is easier said than done: most of us fail miserably many times a day. The maternal spiritual director has a better chance at consistency and success, if only because the parameters of her work are clearly defined, and she can be sure of some respite.

Some of my learnings from motherhood transfer smoothly to the ministry of spiritual direction. Almost automatically I found myself practicing what the authors of *Women's Ways of Knowing* call maternal conversation. Sometimes it is hard to ask the right questions, but I have learned that the wrong ones can kill love and spontaneity. I have learned too that small people feel abandonment, no matter how much they are cherished, and that they can easily persuade themselves that they are unworthy of love. I have learned that gentleness can accomplish a lot more than harshness, although confrontation is fashionable these days.

Mothers provide safety and reassurance even when their confidence is unwarranted. British lay theologian Margaret Hebblethwaite instinctively greeted her first-born, seconds after his birth, with the words, "Dominic Paul, it's all right, it's all right." Upon reflection, she observed that this message of comfort from mother to child is a metaphysical statement.[7] "It's all right"—words probably spoken by mothers as Herod's soldiers searched the houses of Bethlehem for baby boys, by mothers in boxcars en route to death camps, by mothers in all times and all places kissing small hurts to make them well. Not surprisingly, at least one translation of a crucial passage from Julian's *Showings* makes the same metaphysical statement and provides it with a context:

> On one occasion the good Lord said, "Everything is going to be all right." On another, "You will see for yourself that every sort of thing will be all right." In these two sayings the soul discerns various meanings.
>
> One is that he wants us to know that not only does he care for great and noble things, but equally for little and small, lowly and simple things as well. This is his meaning:

*Chapter Four*
WOMEN AND SPIRITUAL DIRECTION

"*Everything* will be all right." We are to know that the least things will not be forgotten.[8]

In their instinctively murmured words of comfort, mothers do not deny the pain, uncertainty, even the terror of life. They simply remind the child—and themselves—that at the deepest level, it is all right. We can do this as spiritual directors, not in false cheeriness or denial, but by our own steadfastness. If *we* believe with Julian that, in spite of everything, it will be all right, we need not say these words. We will embody them.

## Women in Spiritual Direction

I have already noted that the preponderance of those seeking referral to a spiritual director are women. If male clergy and seminarians are excluded, the disproportionate number of women is even more striking. These are almost always women for whom the old ways no longer serve. A generation ago they might have been immersed in traditional "women's work" in the parish, where they would not have expected to hear their experience addressed in sermons nor comprehended by the liturgy. Now they are looking for something more, coming to grips for the first time with a deeper call to ministry—which may be misinterpreted as a call to ordination. The institutional church has not been helpful to these women; while lip-service is paid to the importance of lay ministry, the powerful unspoken message remains: the *real* minister is the one up front on Sunday morning. The power and urgency of the call are unmistakable, and the woman knows that she must do something about it. Left on her own, she can see few paths other than ordination. The spiritual director can assist her in the work of discernment, most importantly by helping her to a broader vision of ministry.

It is easy to be dismissive of the stereotypical "midlife crisis," forgetting the extraordinary promise of this crucial time. Regardless of the nature of their call, these women are to be heard and taken seriously, for they are wrestling with issues of vocation. God is calling them to something. What? Something more than turning up faithfully on Sunday morning, and something more than devoted committee work. But what? They are impelled to move beyond the safety of either traditional parish roles or bland indifference to the risk of embarking on a search for intimacy with God, which may only increase their present loneliness.

I am struck by the isolation of these women. Many are without a life partner, rarely by choice. To some extent, they turn to God in their very human loneliness, but it would be cruelly reductionist to minimize their yearning on this account. Furthermore, I am touched by the spiritual isolation of many married women who seem to have everything—a stable marriage, material possessions in abundance, and community standing. They enter spiritual direction not so much out of greedy desire to add God to their already considerable possessions, but rather from a sense of emptiness. They too deserve to be taken seriously.

It is easy to dismiss women who are obviously needy but inarticulate. Some directors see their yearning for God as pathological and want to pass them on quickly to psychotherapists or marriage counselors, but there is a distinctive quality to a woman's spiritual search that merits attention. Madonna Kolbenschlag observes that women seek advice and counsel much more frequently than men do, and turn to an exploration of their spirituality—indeed, to religion in general—as therapy, sometimes getting stuck in what she calls a "passive-receptive mode."[9] While there is much wisdom in her observations, I would argue that women must be the recipients of healing before they can become its dispensers. While their need for approval may initially be excessive, they can and must grow into the assurance that they are worthy, known, and accepted before they can move on to the next step. It is important that the director, male or female, lay or ordained, be wary of the dangers of getting stuck in dependency even though a time of being ministered to is a necessary first stage.

*Chapter Four*
WOMEN AND SPIRITUAL DIRECTION

When women come seeking spiritual direction, I sense in them a great yearning, regardless of their relative woundedness or health, their zeal or their passivity. They are yearning to be known, to be able to say with Jeremiah, "Yet you, O LORD, are in the midst of us, and we are called by your name" (Jer. 14:9). They are yearning to know that their voice will be heard, but their experience in the church over the centuries has created painful impediments. As I noted in my discussion of women's special qualities as directors, the voices of authority have been traditionally male: preachers, pastors, theologians, confessors, and spiritual directors. As Martin Smith comments in *Reconciliation,*

> The historical monopoly men have had of the official teaching roles in the church, a monopoly now happily on the way to being broken, has meant, among other things, that women have usually been required to understand their relationship with God and their ethical and spiritual responses in terms that do not fit the special dynamics of women's lives.[10]

The exclusion of women has sometimes been the result of benign neglect; more often, however, it reflects contempt, fear, cruelty, and complete disregard of the message of the Gospel. Even now, the most commonly cited studies of faith development and ethical decision-making (Erikson, Fowler, Kohlberg) purport to speak for all, but are based on studies of male experience. On the commonly used scales, most women remain "immature" in their faith development.

By and large, too, traditional acculturation inhibits growth toward true maturity, and women are discouraged from becoming fully themselves. The glorification of the child-woman pervades our culture. With the help of the cosmetics and fitness industries, the mature woman must work hard to remain girlishly youthful, careful not to show her life experience in her face or her body. Yet an even more insidious barrier to maturity is the ideal of living for others. As Joann Wolski Conn observes:

> Christian teaching and practice, instead of promoting women's maturity, has significantly contributed to its restriction. Women have consistently been taught to value only one type of religious development—self-denial and sacrifice of one's own needs for the sake of others. Whereas men have been taught to couple self-denial with prophetic courage to resist undue authority, women have been taught to see all male authority as God-given and to judge that assertion of their own desires was a sign of selfishness and pride.[11]

I know women who accept a life of utter self-effacement without questioning the purpose or the object of the sacrifice. While there are scriptural grounds in support of self-sacrifice, there must first be *a mature self* to sacrifice, and the spiritual director can assist in the development of that self.

## Issues of Language in Directing Women

Traditionally, then, women are not socialized to value themselves, their insights, their opinions, or their questions. Writing about the diffidence of women in a typical academic setting, historian Gerda Lerner notes that in their muteness they are saying: "I do not deserve to take up time and space."[12]

A woman brings this attitude to spiritual direction as well as to the classroom, often arriving with a sense of unworthiness, of not measuring up—although to what, she is not sure. She may feel herself judged by God and thereby face a split between who and where she really is in terms of life experience and deep concerns, and who and where she thinks she should be. This is especially poignant in matters of love and charity, where the directee finds herself taking a softer line than the perceived "right" one. Thus Marilyn came to me wrestling with her conscience: she felt guilty that she was unable to judge gay people harshly, even though her strict religious upbringing had taught her that they merited condemnation. Simply articulating her dilemma, in the safety of our time together, enabled her to stand on her own spiritual feet.

*Chapter Four*
## WOMEN AND SPIRITUAL DIRECTION

Or a woman seeking direction may present herself as tentative and indirect, almost to the point of playing guessing games. The director may be tempted to dismiss her as "not serious" or immature, particularly if he is unaware of the characteristics of women's language.[13] Women who wish to be taken seriously have to become bilingual: they become fluent in the language of the dominant group and suppress their natural speech, at least in "important" conversations. More pervasive and usually unconscious is a verbal tentativeness, an unwillingness to take responsibility for what is said through the frequent use of qualifiers like "rather," "perhaps," or "some." Statements of conviction lose their strength when introduced with "I believe" or "I think" instead of "I know." In order to involve the listener in statements, thus securing his agreement, women may end a sentence interrogatively, either in actual words ("Isn't it?") or by a rising inflection of voice.[14]

Jane was a directee capable of making strong statements and asking powerful questions, and then demolishing them before any response was possible. Her entrapment in "woman's language" made her appear shallow and indecisive, a dilettante. Even when I understood the situation and felt great liking for her, I found myself fighting irritation at the teasing hesitance in her speech. Our work together progressed only when I pointed out to her what I had observed and asked her permission to call to her attention each time she slipped into her familiar pattern. She had been unaware of her tendency toward verbal self-destruction and gratefully agreed to my plan.

The director can and must help by holding a woman responsible for her statements; this means, first of all, assuring her that it is safe to be responsible. I am convinced that much of women's tentative speech arises from fear of her own anger, that somehow there will be terrible retribution—divine or otherwise—if she reveals herself as a strong person. Occasionally I remind Susanne, who is an expert at indirect and hesitant speech, that God already knows her dangerous thoughts and has thus far resisted zapping her, while she has nothing to fear from me. I will be delighted when we have grown sufficiently in love and trust for Susanne to feel safe to rage at God or at me. It's coming, but it is still a long way off.

We need to listen for questions as well, especially for the unasked questions. Women have had little to do with posing the questions or creating the agendas of theology. If Priscilla or Thecla had written our epistles instead of Paul, I suspect there would have been a good deal about the Incarnation and relatively little about circumcision! Consequently, traditional theology often seems to have answers for questions that are never asked and questions for which there are no answers.[15]

## Valuing Experience

It is common for the dominant group to assume that it understands the experience of an oppressed group. Thus white people are surprised when they realize they do not understand the lives of black people; if they are open with trusted black friends who will speak the truth to them, they may be able to approach understanding by way of their imagination. Similarly, there is the assumption that male clergy, preachers, spiritual directors, and confessors understand women's experience because—after all—it isn't really so different. By their unwillingness to value their own experience and their silence concerning it, women have contributed to this fallacy.

Considering how inseparable woman's physical being is from her spirituality, it is striking how much of her bodily experience is taboo for open discussion. Menstruation remains a secret topic, with most public mention in negative terms: does woman's cyclical nature make her unstable and unreliable? Menopause is seen as either comic or pathetic, an exception being Margaret Meade's joyous prayer of thanksgiving for the energy and zest of post-menopausal women. Pregnancy and birth are usually relegated to the women's magazines, despite Luke's exemplary theological treatment of the subject. And rarely addressed, in spiritual

*Chapter Four*
WOMEN AND SPIRITUAL DIRECTION

terms, is women's own deep dislike of their bodies, their dissatisfaction with certain features, and their pervasive sense that they need to lose weight—literally to diminish themselves. Finally, for too many women, their initial sexual experience is experience of violation and abuse. <u>Since women's most powerful and formative experiences are often the hidden, secret ones, they may seem insignificant</u> in the grand scheme of things, and hence <u>too homely for theological reflection</u>.

There are times when a woman will work more fruitfully with another woman, quite possibly a lay woman. After all, women talk differently among themselves, as do men, and a special shared understanding exists between women of common experience. While this does not mean that the directee must be matched with her mirror image, she needs someone to whom all aspects of her experience will be acceptable and understandable. Of course it is equally important to stress that there are many sensitive, imaginative men who meet this requirement. Their very otherness makes them valuable for the woman who is trying to gain a clear perspective. Mindless segregation has no place in spiritual direction, indeed would be a step backward. Men *can* serve as directors for women!

In her fear of seeming trivial and in her undervaluing of her own experience, the directee may avoid topics and areas of deep concern. The spiritual implications of a long and "uneventful" marriage are often unexplored and underrated. The costs and fruits of faithfulness are not always evident, but have a profound effect on the woman's spiritual identity. The spirituality of housework is another neglected area. Most of my male friends and colleagues are unaware of the burden of repetitive menial work that is never done, work that is noticed only when it is neglected. Further, time spent with very young children can simultaneously enrich the spirit, deaden the mind, and tax patience beyond belief. All of this is the raw material of spiritual direction; all of this has a God-component, even though the directee does not see in the minutiae of her life an experience of God.

The director's task is to help the woman find and trust her voice so that her story can be told. To do this is to give her permission to be, discover, and reveal her true self. Here, as always, spiritual direction is a ministry of compassionate presence. The directee must be taken seriously, even when she seems not to take herself seriously. If either male or female directors are to listen critically without pre-judging, it is vital that they know their own biases. For example, some men should not try to work with well-groomed, well-dressed, middle-class and middle-aged women; unable to see beyond these externals, they are too quick to typecast these women as superficial and materialistic. Similarly, an extreme feminist might have little understanding of a dedicated stay-at-home mother, just as the recently divorced woman might see her directee's commitment to a difficult marriage as pathological.

Taking everything seriously, the director never condescends even when the story is told haltingly and without theological sophistication. It is important for director (and directee) to understand that one can talk about "spiritual" matters without a theological vocabulary. The raw material is there: all that is needed is for the directee to trust her own voice. Asking the right questions can clarify and dispel tentativeness, helping the woman to move away from undue dependence on the authority of others and claim her own innate authority, free her submerged self. Parzival released the king from his suffering and brought the entire Grail community into harmony and wholeness when he finally asked the simple question: "Uncle, where do you hurt?" It is such a simple question that the director might forget to ask it, particularly when the woman (or man) sitting opposite seems strong and positive. As traditional caregivers, most women are not prepared for this question, although they would expect it from a physician. Socialized to put their own wishes aside (or at least to disguise them), they see the question as

*Chapter Four*
WOMEN AND SPIRITUAL DIRECTION

an invitation to selfishness or self-indulgence. Instead, it is an invitation to *self*: merely naming the source of hurt can expose it to light and air and thereby bring about healing.

Important as this is in all aspects of a woman's life, it is especially critical in the area of spirituality. As she begins to answer the question candidly, she may reveal—to her own surprise—years of denial and suppressed pain. The cost of faithfulness has been high, as the woman finds herself able to articulate in religious language and imagery her grief at her exclusion.

A supportive director can help the women find her place in the communal Christian story. The writings of Elisabeth Moltmann-Wendel, Phyllis Trible, and Elisabeth Schuessler-Fiorenza are a valuable resource, but even more effective is "simply" reading the gospels with a woman's eye and being attentive to what is rarely addressed in sermons and teaching. I have conducted a number of retreats on "The Women around Jesus."[16] In one of the first gatherings, I ask the retreatants (usually women) to retell from memory the story of the woman who anointed Jesus. Unfailingly, the group effort reproduces Luke's version: "a woman in the city, who was a sinner...stood behind him at his feet, weeping, and began to bathe his feet with her tears and to dry them with her hair. Then she coninued kissing his feet and anointing them with the ointment" (Lk. 7:37-38). Then I remind them of Mark's telling of the story: "A woman came with an alabaster jar of very costly ointment of nard, and she broke open the jar and poured the ointment on his head" (Mk. 14:3-9). We sit for a moment with the picture of these two women, our sisters: the (presumably sexual) sinner crouched weeping on the floor and the unnamed woman standing tall, a prophet anointing a king. Then we smile and weep simultaneously at the irony of Jesus' words: "Wherever the gospel is preached in the whole world, what she has done will be told in memory of her."

Further, the director can encourage both women and men to be comfortable with feminine imagery for God in prayer.

HOLY LISTENING
*The Art of Spiritual Direction*

This may simply be a matter of "giving permission," or it might possibly be a brief recounting of the director's own experience. To reassure the anxious or uncertain, he can point out often-overlooked feminine imagery in Scripture. I like to encourage experimentation and freedom in solitary prayer time, which can often be combined comfortably with traditional corporate worship.

A woman must be willing to embrace risk if she is to push out the boundaries, find her true self and voice, and thereby grow into her own mature spirituality. It is easier not to face the realization that one's icons have become idols and must be put away, not to accept that one's vision of God has been constricted and distorted. Madonna Kolbenschlag speaks of the "moment of atheism," when the woman lets go of her outgrown faith, ceasing to rely on "authorities" and trusting herself.[17] In my own more homely metaphor, she takes off the training wheels and discovers to her amazement that the bicycle remains upright.

*The Eighth Deadly Sin*

From struggling through *Paradise Lost* in freshman English, we "know" that the worst sin is overweening pride. (I would vote for idolatry or greed in our gluttonous society, but Milton speaks for tradition.) The time I have spent listening to women's stories, however, has convinced me that there are distinctly feminine patterns of sinfulness, and pride is not their besetting sin, even though many readily accuse themselves of it. The model of the woman too good to live, the doomed heroine of the nineteenth-century novel, has been internalized with tragic consequences. Women's patterns of sinning are different from men's, and although embracing the role of victim is a way of remaining "sinless," this very willingness to let oneself be hurt or even destroyed is a striking example of an essentially sinful way of being.

Far from being pride, women's distinctive sin is self-contempt. This self-hatred is symbolized by and centered on the body. I have already noted women's dissatisfaction with

*Chapter Four*
WOMEN AND SPIRITUAL DIRECTION

their physical selves; studies have shown this to be a peculiarly feminine preoccupation, and cultural messages reinforce it. Disorders like anorexia and bulimia represent the consequence of self-hatred carried to the extreme. More important still, women's self-contempt manifests itself as an unwillingness to grow and take the risks that growth demands. It is often difficult for women to see that their reluctance to accept maturity is a tacit refusal of adult responsibility. "How can this be?" they ask, as they feel themselves burdened, indeed overwhelmed, by their responsibilities as wives, mothers, employees, and professionals. Yet by over-zealousness in their obligations toward others, especially husbands and children, and a corresponding neglect of themselves, women manage to avoid inner growth. There is no quality of careless abandon to this spiritual irresponsibility; on the contrary, it is grim and confining.

Women's tentativeness is another manifestation of self-contempt, as is an apparent absorption in triviality. Both are a noisy kind of silence, a screen erected—perhaps unconsciously—against clarity. By hesitating to take firm stands or express herself in decisive language, she sends a strong message that she does not deserve to be heard. By letting herself become immersed in trivialities, she sends a message that she does not deserve to be seen, at least not as an aware adult. Furthermore, absorption in trivialities deadens pain, for the woman is too preoccupied to face herself, her human relationships, and—of course—God.

Tentativeness (a kind of clenched-teeth sweet rage) may also result from a mistaken understanding of anger, since women are socialized to believe that anger itself is avoidable and wrong, and that its expression is sinful. (The word "sin" is rare in our secular vocabulary, but the phenomenon is known, dreaded, and punishable.) As a result, a great deal of spiritual energy goes into combatting the "wrong" sin, and the potentially constructive use of anger is neglected. The result is hurtful and destructive to the woman and to those around her. A woman I knew during my nursing home

# HOLY LISTENING
*The Art of Spiritual Direction*

chaplaincy is etched in my mind: Emma spent her last months filled equally with rage and cancer. Her rigid piety made it impossible for her to question God's purpose, let alone express anger. Outwardly sweet and always courteous to her visitors, she made life hell for the uneducated and poorly paid women who were her caretakers. She died without being able to face the deep wells of anger within herself.

Denial of a woman's own authority inevitably manifests itself as passivity, not the passivity of a healthy self open and empty to receive the Holy Spirit, but a leaden inertia. Without discounting the biochemical, genetic, and neurological causes, it seems clear that at least some depression is of spiritual origin. Similarly, the passivity of self-contempt can reveal itself in addictions, the obvious ones of food, pills, and alcohol as well as the less obvious ones of sleep, hyperactivity, and consumerism. The last is especially insidious, since it is culturally reinforced and stimulated.

It is important not to minimize the sin of self-hatred and self-contempt. It is a sin, for at its heart is a denial of God's love and the goodness of God's creation. Pride plays a part after all, for the woman discounts herself as part of creation and assumes that the rules of divine love do not apply to her. That love is there for everyone else, but not for her.

Like all sin, this cannot be private, hurting the sinner alone; instead its ramifications touch others, in the woman's immediate circle and beyond. There is the waste of gifts that have not been used, frequently not even acknowledged, coupled with the inability to receive the gifts of others. Self-contempt is a loveless field that offers prime growing conditions to other sins, among them false humility, envy, manipulativeness, and sloth. Sloth is an especially sneaky sin, since it can disguise itself in busy-ness. Here again, absorption in trivialities is a symptom.

The director's task is to listen and detect patterns of self-deception, for women's ways of sinning depend on obfuscation. My two favorite questions—"What do you want?" and

*Chapter Four*
WOMEN AND SPIRITUAL DIRECTION

"Where do you hurt?"—are excellent diagnostic tools for getting at sinful ways at being and at the same time revealing the innate beauty and goodness the woman denies. The director, however, must guard against joining her in trivializing herself. A sense of sin is to be taken seriously, for it is a heavy burden on the directee. It is no comfort to be told, "Oh, that's not really very important," or worse still, to be dismissed with a patronizing smile. Even when a sense of sin is misplaced or misguided, it is a sign that something is wrong. Many women come to spiritual direction prepared, even eager, to believe the worst about themselves. The shame caused by the injuries they have endured is easily confused with their own personal guilt.

Some women suffer from a pervasive sense of guilt and sin simply because they exist. This is rarely conscious or articulated, but it is crippling. The most striking example in my experience came in a conversation with Grace, an intelligent woman of great probity, whose jealous supervisor had accused her of financial wrongdoing in the management of her department. Almost in despair she protested, "I didn't do it. I never even thought about the possibilities for corruption. I know she's crazy. So why do I feel so guilty?" Similarly, Allie found herself singled out for small, cruel practical jokes by a member of the custodial staff of her school. Instead of openly expressed anger, her response was acceptance of her own guilt: "I must have done something; I must have hurt him somehow." Even more tragically, the phenomenon of victims of rape and sexual abuse who blame themselves is well documented.

Avoiding both harshness and condescension, the director can help the woman separate the strands of her sinfulness. The author of *The Cloud of Unknowing* aptly observes that sin is "a lump"; we need to differentiate the lump and understand its chemical composition, for very likely it contains a lot of inert matter and perhaps even something of value. The director assists in separating the good from the bad, the significant from the insignificant. It is delicate and gentle work,

HOLY LISTENING
*The Art of Spiritual Direction*

for <u>sin always involves hurt</u>: hurt of others, hurt of God, hurt of oneself.

*Survivors of Abuse*

The whole area of sexuality and sexual experience is a delicate one. Directees are often reluctant to bring this material to spiritual direction—whether it is sexual orientation, rape, incest, illegitimate births, or abortions—and it may take a long time for the real issues to surface. For both director and directee, this is a time of testing. When I sense that much is left unsaid and a great piece of the picture is missing, I probe a little: "Tell me about your family" or "Do you live alone?" I must be prepared for disappointment; such inquiries may not lead anywhere, at least initially. The directee may not exhibit the discomfort that often accompanies denial or evasion: there is simply no information forthcoming.

The directee naturally wonders, "Will I be accepted? Or shamed?" Sometimes she asks this question directly, as Beth did in our first meeting: "I'm a lesbian. Is that going to bother you?" I assured her it wouldn't, but also invited her to let me know if, at any point, *I* bothered *her*. Of course, the deeper and still unspoken question is, "Does God accept me?" This is no occasion for politeness. It is a good rule not to accept a directee if you cannot be compassionate, and hence are in danger of making judgments or showing contempt.

In the past decade scientific studies and first-hand accounts of sexual abuse have proliferated. It is now commonly accepted that one woman in four has been violated: this can range from rape to isolated instances of improper touch or fondling. (Verbal violation, still mistakenly believed by some men to be flattering to a woman, is not included.) One woman in ten is the victim of ongoing sexual abuse, but this is a conservative figure. While there are male victims of sexual abuse, this is typically a crime and sin against female children. The myth of the dangerous stranger is just that: the

*Chapter Four*
WOMEN AND SPIRITUAL DIRECTION

woman who has been sexually abused is usually the victim of a known and trusted person—her father (most often), uncle, grandfather, mother's "boyfriend," or brother. In sibling incest there is a *slight* possibility that the relationship is consensual; usually it is coercive. Even though the coercion is not always physical, it is an act of spiritual and emotional violence.

Over the past five years, I have seen increasing numbers of women who have survived incest. They are a special group among my directees, with a distinctive spirituality. These survivors seem drawn to the church. Sometimes, they tell me, it was the only safe place in a nightmarish childhood. Sometimes they experience real grace through a sense of God's love, in spite of everything. I would be reluctant to dismiss their devotion to the church as denial or compensation, although it is undeniable that religion can be used to escape reality.

When some incest survivors come to spiritual direction, they are genuinely unaware of their own painful history. Because their memories are too overwhelming, amnesia is a means of survival. Years of incest and rape are not a part of their consciousness until, in middle age, they begin to recall. Memory may return gradually or suddenly. At this point, spiritual direction is not enough; it is only one component in the woman's work toward wholeness. She urgently needs psychotherapeutic help from a specially trained person, or one who is highly sensitive to issues of sexual abuse. There are also support groups and twelve-step programs; these can be helpful after a period of intensive individual psychotherapy or in conjunction with it, and I am comfortable working in cooperation with the psychotherapist, with directee acting as go-between. Unless the directee initiates it, I have no actual contact with the psychotherapist. (I have never met Linda's therapist, for example, but I feel great affection and respect for her. Linda regularly conveys our greetings to each other.)

# HOLY LISTENING
*The Art of Spiritual Direction*

Before recalling the painful memories, the abuse survivor may seem to be functioning adequately. But she may also seem talkative, even shallow; her preoccupation with triviality is like a bandage covering her painful wound.[18] Or she may have been drawn instinctively to the pain of others, hence much concerned with "good works" and "helping others." Here the director needs to be patient, allowing time for trust to build up. Even as they reach out for support and understanding, there is no reason for these women to trust *anyone*. For the most part survivors are skilled at coping on a superficial level, but a long time is required to get past courteous banalities.

Unless the director knows where to look, there is often no obvious clue to the pain and inner turmoil. I am developing a sixth—and at this point indefinable—sense of the special woundedness of the sexually abused. However, it is especially important to tread softly if the person is in a state of amnesia; and I may know intuitively much more than I need or should articulate to the directee. At most, I permit myself a gentle invitation to go deeper: "I sense that you have been hurt a lot."

When the directee has begun to recall her earlier experience, there is a continued need for patience. As more material surfaces, the direction relationship grows in trust, and the directee moves toward some kind of healing. Sometimes it feels as if we are gradually peeling off layers of concealment; at others, it is like going ever deeper down a spiral staircase. As in all direction relationships, but here especially, confidentiality must be impeccable. The victim is filled with shame, and almost always suffers the typical confusion of guilt and shame: she feels somehow to blame for what was done to her. As she moves toward greater healing and its concomitant awareness, she is frightened by glimpses of her own deep rage and her fear of what might happen if that rage were expressed.

In working with survivors of sexual abuse, there are no short cuts. The spiritual director must scrupulously avoid

*Chapter Four*
## WOMEN AND SPIRITUAL DIRECTION

"shoulds" and "oughts," with one great exception. I remember saying to Linda, "Most of the time, I will be careful not to tell you what you should do. But there is one thing you *must* do, and I will keep at you about it: value yourself!" The survivor feels devalued and sullied; she cannot be told too often that she is worthy of love and respect. (At my suggestion, Linda took as her mantra, "I am clean!" She wove the words into her prayers, taped them on her mirror, and clung to them when shame threatened to flood over her.)

Occasionally I receive referrals from psychotherapists. If it is in accordance with her religious tradition, a therapist may feel a survivor might be helped by the sacrament of reconciliation. These are poignant confessions, not to be hurried. Even though she knows intellectually that she was betrayed and violated, the woman feels compelled to blame herself. Moreover, she is sure that the rage welling up in her is a confirmation of her sinfulness. We talk about her anger and how it can be a source of sin or great constructive energy. The woman has undoubtedly already heard this from her psychotherapist, but it is good news when told afresh in a religious setting. Technically, I should withhold absolution because I have heard the story of the victim, not the perpetrator, but this is not the time for a legalistic approach to the sacraments. The woman's relief is almost palpable when I place my hands on her head and say, "The Lord has put away all your sins. Go in peace." I will probably never see her again.

The greatest gift the director can bring is a loving presence. While it is important to maintain detachment, a deep emotional involvement is also inevitable and desirable. I have already told of Linda's response to my tears, which I had hoped to whisk away before she could see them. As memories come flooding back, the director may hear of horror and degradation beyond belief, and at such times, I break my rule about limiting conversations between regular meetings. I invited one woman to call me at any time, day or night, until this particularly painful period had been lived

# HOLY LISTENING
*The Art of Spiritual Direction*

through. She accepted the invitation, but never abused my hospitality.

Spiritual directors, women or men, need to find some way of dealing with their own reactions to the painful material. If they themselves have experienced abuse, they may be tempted to identify too closely with the directee, even to the point of appropriating the other's pain. On the other hand, if they have had warm, healthy relationships with their families, it may be difficult for them to believe that families are capable of intentional cruelty toward their most helpless members. In any event, dealing with her own emotions is a delicate process for a woman spiritual director, because the directee's confidences must be protected. Conversation with her own director can help restore perspective, so long as she is careful to concentrate on her own reactions and not on the raw material of the survivor's story. Writing in a journal is invaluable, as is prayer—both for those who trust her and for herself. I realize that when I pray for Linda she has become for me a symbol of all women and children suffering abuse.

Here again there are no short cuts, because this can be heavy, lonely work. After doing spiritual direction with a number of abuse survivors, I know things that I would rather not know, and I have glimpsed depths whose existence I would prefer to deny. Yet at all times the director needs to be credulous. We are still suffering from Freud's failure to believe the real experiences of upper-middle-class girls in turn-of-the-century Vienna. <u>If the directee said it happened, it happened</u>. And it is still happening: even after decades of amnesia, flashes of recollection have an almost unbearable immediacy.

Although some men can be vulnerable and compassionate listeners to these painful stories, there are also many men who do not want to know about the abuse of women. It may be impossible, therefore, for a man to work with an abused woman, at least in the early stages of her growing awareness. One directee, whose appearance and manner gives no clue to her painful history, has told me of her difficulty at the ex-

*Chapter Four*
## WOMEN AND SPIRITUAL DIRECTION

change of the Peace during the Eucharist; for a long time, she tried to position herself so that she would not have to touch or be touched by a man. It is not surprising that she and other survivors would be ill at ease with a male director, although gay men, who themselves have received societal abuse, often have surprising rapport with survivors of incest. It must be difficult for compassionate men not to take this rejection personally. At later stages, their supportive male presence can greatly advance healing, but until then they must be content to wait.

The survivors of sexual abuse have a difficult task of integration. Understandably, they are even more likely than others to fall prey to the common tendency to separate the "spiritual" from what has really happened in their lives. God-talk may either be infrequent or else voluble but disconnected from reality. In either case, I ask from time to time: "Where was God when this was happening to you? Where is God now? Do you feel angry with God?" They are often afraid to express the possibility of anger, having a tendency to excuse God as if God's attention had merely wandered during their ordeal. Along with this unwillingness to face squarely the presence or absence of God, most abuse survivors are just as reluctant to confront the probable complicity of their mothers. At least in the early stages of work, it is more bearable to see the father (or brother, uncle, or grandfather) as acting in isolation. Eventually they come to share the insight of Elie Wiesel and other Holocaust survivors whose faith was forged in suffering: God was there, in the suffering.

These are courageous women. I have learned a great deal about prayer from them. The psalms are a source of strength for them, especially Psalm 22 ("My God, my God, why have you forsaken me? and are so far from my cry and from the words of my distress") and Psalm 88 ("O Lord, my God, my Savior, by day and night I cry to you"). The imprecatory psalms are often a surprise to women schooled in niceness; I encourage them to read and savor the angry parts. For ex-

# HOLY LISTENING
*The Art of Spiritual Direction*

ample, these verses of Psalm 69 are a fine example of unbridled rage:

> Let the table be a trap for them
>   a snare for their allies.
> Let their eyes be darkened so that they cannot see,
>   and make their loins tremble continually.
> Pour out your indignation upon them,
>   and let your burning anger overtake them.
> May their camp be a desolation;
>   let no one live in their tents (vv. 22-25).

If the Psalmist could urge God to wreak terrible vengeance on his adversaries, the survivor of abuse can permit herself a little anger. She can write it, speak it, or shout it.

I encourage prayers of petition for understanding, strength, and restored health. But I am very cautious about the danger of prematurity in prayers of forgiveness. Again and again, the survivor says, "I know I should forgive my father, but...." Or even more painfully, "My mother and the whole family tell me that I should be willing to forgive and forget." The wound of abuse is like any other deep and infected wound. If the surface is allowed to heal over too quickly, poison remains to spread sickness deep within. So I counsel the directee to pray to want to be able to forgive—some day.

I have already touched upon the healing power of sacramental confession, even when the penitent is more burdened by shame than by guilt. It is helpful for the director to point out the difference, in no way minimizing the tremendous burden of shame. The privacy of the confessional might be the only place where the directee feels safe to articulate it and to dispel its power by naming it directly. It helps restore perspective when I ask, "Where is your sin in this?" Or "Where is the potential for sin?" Both are there, but rarely in the ways assumed by the abuse survivor.

It goes without saying that I am cautious about paternal imagery in prayer, for example, in the use of the Our Father. To avoid the possibility of unwittingly inflicting more pain

*Chapter Four*
WOMEN AND SPIRITUAL DIRECTION

upon her, I am willing to be led by the directee, who may either find in God the loving father whom she has not known on earth, or who may prefer to separate herself as far as possible from all parental imagery.

Finally, the woman who has survived sexual abuse often develops into a powerful intercessor. It does not happen easily or quickly: at first she must deal intensively with her own experiences, then with those of women and children whose suffering has been similar. As she perseveres, she often finds in herself wells of compassion for *all* victims.

# Endnotes

1 Mary Field Belenky et al., *Women's Ways of Knowing* (New York: Basic Books, 1986), p. 48.

2 *Ibid.*, p. 184.

3 Simone Weil, *Waiting for God* (New York: Harper Colophon, 1973), pp. 146-147.

4 Belenky, *Knowing*, p. 189.

5 Sandra M. Schneiders, "Effects of Women's Experience on Spirituality," in Giles, p. 34.

6 *Ibid.*, pp. 34-35.

7 Margaret Hebblethwaite, *Motherhood and God* (London: Geoffrey Chapman, 1984), pp. 31-33.

8 Julian of Norwich, p. 109.

9 *Madonna Kolbenschlag, Kiss Sleeping Beauty Goodbye* (San Francisco: Harper & Row, 1988), pp. 181ff.

10 Martin Smith, *Reconciliation* (Cambridge, MA: Cowley, 1985), p. 77. See also J. Neville Ward, *The Following Plough* (Cambridge, MA: Cowley, 1984), p. 94.

11 Joann Wolski Conn, ed., *Women's Spirituality: Resources for Christian Development* (New York: Paulist, 1986), p. 4.

12  Gerda Lerner, *The Majority Finds Its Past* (New York: Oxford University Press, 1979), pp. 243-44. Similarly, Carol Gilligan notes that women are unwilling to make moral judgments, feeling that they have no right to do so. Thus they exclude themselves from decision-making (*In A Different Voice*, pp. 16ff).

13  In addition to my own observations, I am greatly indebted to Robin Lakoff's small but seminal book, *Language and Woman's Place* (New York: Harper Torchbooks, 1975).

14  Lakoff observes that this intonational pattern is found in English only among women speakers. (*Language and Woman's Place*, p. 17).

15  The authors of *Women's Ways of Knowing* note a similar phenomenon in secular higher education: "The courses are about the culture's questions, questions fished out of the 'mainstream' of the disciplines. If the student is female, her questions may differ from the culture's questions, since women, paddling in the bywaters of the culture, have had little to do with positing the questions or designing the agendas of the disciplines" (p. 198).

16  Elisabeth Moltmann-Wendel's book of the same title provided the stimulus.

17  Kolbenschlag, *Sleeping Beauty*, pp. 185-87.

18  Otherwise sympathetic writers judge women severely if not harshly for their "triviality," failing to see that it can be a means of coping, even survival. For examples, see J. Neville Ward, *The Following Plough*, p. 100, and Martin Smith, *Reconciliation*, p. 78.

# Epilogue

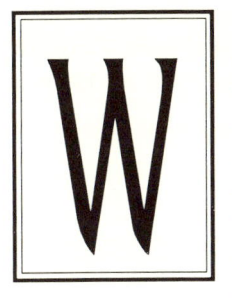

Writing a book about spiritual direction is a presumptuous act: one sets oneself up as an authority. Perhaps one is even taken seriously and becomes raw material for footnotes! Yet I am still working on my definition of spiritual direction, playing with images and models, and ever more aware that whatever a spiritual director is—I am not quite there yet. Increasingly, I rejoice in my amateur status and pray God that I never lose it.

The amateur is a lover. Love impels her work and lies at its heart. Spiritual direction, as a work of love, is also a work of freedom. The director is willing to let be, to love with an open hand. Hers is a contemplative love, immune from temptation to devour, possess, or manipulate. Always seeing the other as a child of God, she is filled with respect, even awe in the presence of the person sitting across the sacred space—be it my holy patch of worn carpet or the other end of a park bench.

Willing to let go and let be, the director is unwilling to despair. He has faith in the process of growth and change— and even more faith in the power of God's grace. This is a ministry of hope and newness that enlivens, and even helps define, the status of the amateur. The professional works according to standard procedures; when I visit my ophthalmologist or my dentist for a regular examination, I have come to know the routine. But when I spend an hour in spiritual direction, I am much less certain what will happen. Even in the security and comfort of a long-standing relationship, with well-established rhythms and rituals, each meeting is a new beginning. The amateur-director must be ready for the unexpected; despite all our attempts at domestication, God deals in surprises--a fact most of us don't really like.

Since the days of Abraham, God's messengers have had a way of turning up in unlikely places and at unlikely times. When I read Luke's account of the Annunciation and manage to put aside the pretty pictures that clutter my imagination, I am astonished by the overwhelming terror of this story of the inbreaking of the unexpected. Luke tells us that Mary was "greatly troubled" at the angel's greeting—and well she might be! What a masterpiece of understatement! Mary might have preferred an ordinary day, a placid period of betrothal, followed by marriage to Joseph and a nice, ordinary family. Instead she received a momentous greeting.

The Annunciation is the story of ultimate surprise: God's messenger breaks into the routine of the ordinary and the predictable, and announces the divine presence among and within us. Sometimes I ask myself and my directees, What would you do if an angel were waiting in the back seat of your car, or in your office, or at home in your kitchen? You, with a deadline to meet, or a spouse who is demanding a little space in your life, or a sick child, or a critical encounter with your boss looming up in the very near future. Or perhaps you are tired, at the edge of burnout, and plan to spend two or three glorious hours letting your mind go pleasantly numb before the TV. And you hear: "Hail, O favored one, the Lord is with you. Have I got something for you!"

Spiritual direction is about entertaining these troublesome and unpredictable angels who turn up at surprising and rarely convenient times and places. More importantly, spiritual direction is about recognizing those angels and helping our sisters and brothers who entrust themselves to us to be joyously attentive to those small annunciations that don't always seem like good news. Indeed, they may look like blows or set-backs, interruptions and intrusions into our tidy, well-planned lives. Occasionally the news is joyous and clear, but the annunciation can take the form of downright bad news: illness, rejection, bereavement, seeming loss and waste.

The God who surprises uses strange, unlikely, even dubious material—including those of us who practice the ministry of spiritual direction. The God who surprises wastes nothing, including our "mistakes." I look back on incidents caused by my own ineptness, graciously rescued and transformed, with the gratitude and amazement felt by one who has unconsciously danced on the edge of an abyss. Again and again, I am struck by the power of this ministry, made fruitful by our mutual faithfulness and by God's economy. Words that seemed to me banal and inadequate at the time have had meaning for the directee, while silence born of my incompetence has become rich and deep. Then I remember the fearsome Mrs. G of my hospital ministry, her dismissal of me as an agent of change, my summary relegation to amateur status: "You mean you just walk around and listen to people?" More than host, teacher, or midwife, as a spiritual director I am a holy listener.

*Listen* is such a little, ordinary word that it is easily passed over. Yet we all know the pain of not being listened to, of not being heard. I feel a clutch at my heart whenever I see a child who is desperate, inarticulate with grief, crying for his preoccupied parent to listen to him. My vicarious anguish seems excessive until I realize that I am that child fearing the awful emptiness when a voice goes unheard. Munch and Siquieros have captured this terrible isolation in their paintings, and all of us, if we delve into memory, have experienced it.

In a way, not to be heard is not to exist. This can be the plight of the very young and the very old, the very sick, the "confused," and all too frequently the dying—literally no one in their lives has time or patience to listen. Or perhaps we lack courage to hear them. As time-obsessed people, we dismiss those not "worth" listening to. By contrast, the holy listener is reluctant to dismiss another person; as an amateur who is open to surprises, he makes a willing gift of his attentiveness. At present, this gift is all too rare, as spiritual direc-

# HOLY LISTENING
*The Art of Spiritual Direction*

tors remain in short supply. Many people have found a substitute in psychotherapy: ironically, ours is the first culture that pays others to listen to us. Perhaps it is time for amateurs to reclaim their calling.

We forget how intimate listening is, alive and fluid in its mutuality. It involves interaction even if no one moves a muscle and even if the listener says nothing. Vulnerability is shared when silence is shared.

Holy listening is a work of mutual obedience. It is important to remember the link between listening and the much maligned and misunderstood virtue of obedience: to be obedient is to listen, to hear. It bears no relation to Pavlovian reflexes or to cringing servility. Both the director and the directee are listening and hearing, attentive and respectful. Spiritual directors can find a model in the story of child Samuel and the priest Eli (Sam. 3:1-18). It is comforting to remember that Eli—who is wise, experienced, and attentive—nevertheless misses the point twice, but the Lord keeps on calling. Both Eli and Samuel, director and directee, are enmeshed in listening—each to his truest self, to the other, and ultimately to God.

We can be Eli's for our directees. We can listen and help them listen for the voice of God in Scripture, dreams, the words of friends and enemies, to hear "what they knew all along." We can encourage them to go trustfully into a dark place and to wait: Go, lie down, and if he calls you, you shall say, "Speak, Lord, for thy servant hears." We can listen with them in darkness, suffering, and solitude, and help them understand what they have heard. Eli guided Samuel at great cost to himself. It is unlikely that the ministry of spiritual direction will make such drastic demands on its practitioners, but we would do well to emulate Eli in his willingness to put self aside.

When both director and directee are mutually obedient and engaged in holy listening, the story gets told. Too often we become isolated both from our own story and the Christian story and become preoccupied with our afflictions or

144

our relationships or our work. Separated from our true context, we can be overcome by our present situation—even when it is basically "good" and when we feel that God has called us to it. I have known seminarians to be inundated by tasks and deadlines; superficially they are performing well, but they have lost touch with themselves and the voice that called them.

Separated from our stories, we lose our identity. In my initial days as chaplain in the nursing home, I despaired of ever distinguishing one patient from another. Old and frail, propped up or strapped into wheelchairs, they lined the long corridors of the skilled nursing floors. Like prisoners and refugees, they all looked alike. I became able to see them as persons, children of God, only when I was willing to be a holy listener and to be present at their sometimes halting and incoherent telling of the story.

As a holy listener—the listening is holy, I am still me—I have to put myself out of the way, to become humble in the true sense of knowing my place in the order of God's creation. I must be disinterested, critical without being judgmental. And above all, I must be reverent, for I am entrusted with something precious and tender. As the stories are told, the vulnerability of both director and directee is apparent as masks fall off or are put aside. The director is invited to share in pain, hunger, courage, hope, joy, and holiness.

The holy listener is also subject to a variety of temptations. I feel I must always have a wise response; must understand, evaluate, and interpret *everything*; must keep the conversation lively as if a spiritual direction meeting were a sacred cocktail party; and—most insidious of all—must be interesting. Once I was simultaneously touched and amused by a note from a directee who thanked me for my "blessed centeredness"; filled with ego-laden performance anxiety, I had feared he found me only hopelessly dull!

Above all, the holy listener is open to anything the directee might bring. She is willing to hear about darkness and desolation, the times of God's seeming absence and neglect.

# HOLY LISTENING
*The Art of Spiritual Direction*

She is not frightened by another's anger, doubt, or fear, and she is comfortable with tears. <u>This ministry of presence is a living out of intercessory prayer,</u> <u>as the holy listener waits and watches.</u> Sometimes the listening takes place in the warmth of the stable, sometimes in the pure white light on the high mountain apart, sometimes in desolation at the foot of the cross, and sometimes with fear and great joy in the encounter with the risen Christ.